Your Only Choice Is to Become Rich!

Skip Flanagan

YOUR ONLY CHOICE IS TO BECOME RICH!

Library of Congress Control Number:	2021914897
Paperback:	978-1-955231-33-6
eBook:	978-1-955231-34-3
Hardcover:	978-1-955231-35-0

Printed in the United States of America

BookChambers®
626 Wilshire Boulevard, Los Angeles
California, 90017
https://thebookchambers.com/
+1-866-250-2223

Table of Contents

Your Only Choice Is to Become Rich!

Proven to Be
The best of both worlds,
knowledgeable of the fact that I have
enemies on both sides. Such are the
extremes of this world.
Good and bad. Peace and war.
Heaven and hell. God and the devil.
Cold or hot. Guilty or innocent.
Right or wrong?

About the Author

Having had a taste of success at many intervals in my life, I am now positioned to be the recipient of success once again. With the God-given talent of being able to write, I am now summoned to prove this very point. Yet if you read my first book and believed, this would have been easily foreseeable. Success is a given, and destiny is earned.

This will definitely be a treat and, yes, a challenge for the rest of my life. I have eclipsed a major hill and obstacle: being able to finish two books. I guess with all the bad things that have happened in my life, the thought of publishing a book and becoming a successful writer seemed hopeless, which made this process very difficult.

I am sincere about change, my destiny, my intentions, and my dreams. I invited you into my life so that you could grow with me. Thanks for continuing to be a part of my family. I know you will enjoy the fictional novels and movies that I'm working on. Trust me, if you're like me, keep reading because I know my writing can only improve your thinking. It can help give you insights to things you may be able to change.

My writing may even assist you in your quest to become a political leader. As I stated in my first book, many Americans are alike, but being American is so hard to do. I'm just like you, a citizen wanting the American dream. I am now positioned to be the recipient of this great dream. I can only smile as my ways and means are those that are morally and spiritually correct in the eyes of God. Also, during quiet times of reflection, I always think and look at all my accomplishments. To this day, every step of my life has been a difficult one. Even so, the majority of those steps were in one accord with God. My fear of failing and the thought of doing something that might compromise my place in heaven were my motivation.

Materially, if you were to attempt to evaluate my accomplishments, you would once again miss and not understand the magnitude of God's use for me. You would miss and not see that God that is also in you. Just like Kodak, proof is in the picture. Yet in this case proof is testament of the response that I received from my first book. Proof is the existence of another book of knowledge that I can be proud of, positioned to touch hearts here in America and abroad.

After all the struggle and setbacks, I'm still American. Still a writer. I still have a possibility of becoming rich. I know how easy it is to just lie down and quit. I'm not a quitter, and I'm unafraid. I have only one choice. That choice is to keep going through this jungle. I have nothing to lose. My only choice is to become rich.

My Ambition

My thoughts are those of love,
And of joy and courage.

My intentions are to bring change,
show truth, not to discourage.

My heart often speaks truths in some
minds, just an inquisition.

My desire to show, to guide all hearts
and minds into a better position.

My ears hear things that I, an American, tend
to not be receptive to.

In and out the other ear as I attempt to
bring to the people a new

Way of thinking. Way of acting. Way to
respect. Way to live.

Yet given this world, things of this nature
are things of dreams, much too hard to give.

Keeps me wandering. Keeps me crying. Keeps me
hoping that someone would just listen.

Steadily falling on deaf ears. In silent prayer.
My dreams. My ambitions.

Skip Flanagan

When I finished my first book, I didn't know what might be the result of my efforts. As an African American, I had a lot to think about. Furthermore, there are many diversions to success. I'm no different from any other American. I worry about how people perceive my beliefs. I worry about Big Brother. Yet I continue to push forward as if there are no outside forces or diversions that are out there. As I look at Bill Clinton and observe how individuals attempt to destroy him with no signs of remorse, it scares me.

I can honestly say that I believe that Americans are for truth. Americans are for justice. Americans are for change. Americans are for peace. I don't know some of America's leaders, and therefore I question some of their motives and intents. Why do we have a Republican Party and a Democratic Party? As far as I know, the Democratic Party is supposed to be for African Americans and those middle-class individuals who want economic parity, those individuals who want to end racism and discourage racial division.

Democratic is synonymous with *American*. Do you remember the Rainbow Coalition? Do you remember John F. Kennedy? Do you know Bill Clinton? The Republican Party is supposed to be for the rich. The Republican Party fights for lower taxes. They want to abolish social programs such as food stamps and welfare. They promote the perfect world concept. Money is the root of their party platform. Wealthy individuals such as George Bush and the actor made president, Ronald Reagan, are Republicans.

When I look at past politicians, I think of Jimmy Carter. He continues to this day to promote peace and be involved with politics. He is committed to do what is right for America and the world, regardless of race, creed, or color. The love for everyone exists. The fear of God exists. A spot in heaven is inevitable for

Jimmy Carter. God cannot be in the heart of some politicians. I think that it is foolish for me to think that everyone believes in God. It is even more foolish to believe that all Democrats are truly Democrats. God is in the hearts of everyone.

Yet the complexity of keeping God with you is difficult when you think of the many means by which evil can eradicate God's presence in an individual. I can only assume that the thought of death, and the thought that an individual is not ready to address the Maker, is justification for that individual's willingness to partner with the forces of evil and attempt to delay this meeting and its consequences. Thus, we attempt to disregard life principles and biblical teachings. Maybe we even raise doubt about the importance of this book of principals inspired and commissioned by God. People may use it when it best suits their individual agendas or purposes. Amid the confusion and the debate, we view puppets or politicians who continue to repeat history.

I see the continual nonexistence of God, the nonexistence of a solid structure and good judgment. It's the same judgment that has imprisoned so many African Americans—not God's judgment, but man's continuous judgment. Man's ability to conform the law and persuade public opinion on his behalf. Consistency does not come in the form of judgments because each individual goes through change each day. A change of heart occurs constantly. Patience and research bring about justice. Justice comes in the form of undying faith and a willingness to accept the consequences of all one's actions, even those actions that one has no control over. Understand that justice is the accumulation of blessings that God will now comfort you with. Yet this comfort might not be seen in public view. God must be present in my life, throughout the duration of my known existence. Let it be known that I fear God and commit fully to do his duty. Whatever that duty may be, wherever God may send me, I ask only that God be with me as I stumble into unexpected crossroads of hell. I trust that together we can work out any situation.

If death is the result of my duty to God, then I will go as a soldier awakened by this introduction to death, eager to reap the benefits of sacrifice and faithfulness, and ready for the challenge and tests of my faithfulness once again. In this world, as I know it will be in others, there is a struggle. To know one exists is a struggle, and to know where others exist is further complicated. Knowledge will always command time and energy, creating work and duty to God.

In America, each day is a struggle. A struggle to be oneself. A struggle to be American. A struggle to be one with God. A struggle to be truthful with individuals who have been less than truthful with you. How can you be truthful and not hurt a friend's feelings? Tell a lie, I guess—or better yet, say nothing at all. What if I said that all Whites were racist? That's a lie. I know it is. Yet to thrive and survive in my community, what would you do? I choose to keep God front and center. What if I said that all Blacks are examples of God's chosen people? I would once again say that this is false. We are all individual Americans with dreams, and we are unsure of our final destiny. The majority of us want what is right for all Americans, for all of the world. However, we are unable to control the hearts of all the power-hungry individuals in this same America. That power postpones one's duty to consistently serve God. Diversions gives one a false sense of being God.

I'm just a quiet observer. I'm patiently observing the hypocrisy, ridding myself of these same tendencies as a relatively young adult. I'm positioning myself to one day serve my country and God. If mayor is where I must serve, then so be it. If president of the United States of America is an option after all this house cleansing, and after all these allies against God are defeated, then so be it. You see, it's not at all improbable that God skips a whole generation, skips all the politicians of this era. What if none of these politicians go to heaven? Who would care? I just pray that when I get my opportunity to be president, I don't succumb to other powers.

Hopefully, everything will be cleared up at the top so we can begin the real process of peace, thereby diverting our efforts to space exploration and the perfection of democracy. That will lead to the need for more family-oriented individuals and bring awareness to the needs of senior citizens. We can incorporate into our agenda a systematic system of preparation and care for the old. We can implement the success of such a program into a world market and make medicine and nursing a multi-trillion-dollar industry. This will further create the need for construction of lavish retirement homes and sustain job after job after job. This will enable the United States to be crowned "the health don of the world. It is a service that demands compensation.

Skip Flanagan for president, 2016. Peace.

You Have Only One Choice

As I now began to assume my place as an adult, I must first evaluate my position as an American citizen. In America, our country operates based on a system of government called a "free democracy. A democracy is a government where the power is bestowed in the people. The people have the authority to make laws and rules that are in the best interest of the people. These rules are implemented so that each individual can pursue happiness without any unlawful injustices and political restraints.

It is a system of government that allows individuals to create their own wealth. It is a government that also creates jobs. The occasional governmental intervention is necessary to stimulate the economy and encourage consumer spending. Jobs that are offered in this country are relatively high-paying jobs, where one can afford an all the luxuries in this life. What can this life afford me? People have dreams of how they want their lives to take shape. Everyone has a vision of his or her dream home, dream car, and dream spouse. The standards for these dreams are established by each individual's role models, those people whom one shares similar taste with, those individuals whom one admires.

All people wish that they were rich, in terms of monetary worth. A million dollars could make it possible to buy most of one's dream materials. It may even get one closer to finding their dream spouse. Most jobs cannot or will not pay a million-dollar salary. Most athletes, actors, and coaches are the exception to this theory. During this lifetime, one is promised nothing more than opportunity. Jobs are available for the qualified. The level of each individual's education usually determines one's financial worth. However, the job hunt is not as simple as one might think, given the fact that all dollars in circulation are accounted for.

Individuals find it difficult to get the dollars to fall in their courts—an abundance of these dollars, I might add. We now understand that the government is an integral part in our lives as we attempt to pursue happiness. We ask ourselves, "How can we participate in this dream life?" We additionally ask, "How can we get a piece of this pie?" I believe it's important to understand what you're getting. You get what you pay for. Minimum-wage jobs afford you a simple lifestyle. Unless you hit the lottery, the prospect of you accumulating a million dollars is very slim.

In reality, there is no chance of owning a Mercedes Benz, a luxury automobile of choice. There is no realistic possibility of owning a plush mansion. These are assets that are reserved for the rich and highly educated. Minimum-wage jobs are usually held by individuals with shortcomings and low levels of education. However, minimum-wage jobs can be held by individuals in transition to high-paying jobs, such as individuals who are in school or those planning for the big transition to riches. Still, the reality is that if you don't get yourself together, if you don't further your education, then the simple life is all that can be expected from minimum wage. These are called entry-level jobs, and they give entry-level pay.

Government jobs can usually afford you a middle-class lifestyle. You won't be rich, but you won't be poor either. Yes, you can afford the Mercedes. Yes, you can afford the big house. Yes you can enjoy fancy foods and buy fancy clothes. These are good jobs. With all jobs, you must be qualified to be hired. Most jobs do not allow you to have a criminal record. This usually spells disqualification for most minority citizens. Given the number of minorities in prison or on probation and parole, this creates a situation where minorities are excluded from most government jobs. This leaves minorities with low-income jobs and low standards of living, which increases the opportunities for crime and mischief, feeding the jail system and making life dangerous for other minorities. It also creates more jobs for those not on probation. Can you see how this thing works? Making no mistakes can bring lots of money.

Plenty of education can bring lots of money. No injustices or oppression allows lots of money. Yet after further research, I've found that White Americans are affected by the same legislation. I have limited my scope on the problems. I now feel a greater need to reach out and simplify this problem by directing solutions toward listening countryman, even those who may not be minorities. Individuals who are simply admirers. Individuals who are in need and seek the knowledge and understanding that I, an American, can give. Well, I have some education. I was on probation and feel as if the system has served me some injustices. Nonetheless, my research has yielded me an avenue to become rich.

That avenue is my religious disposition, my family history, patience, persistence, faith, and consistency in what I believe. I have faith in this very US system of government, this system of capitalism, this democracy. This system allows me to try, fail, and then try again. I have faith in my reliance on self. My life as an entrepreneur.

I have to take some things as given. The fact that a government job is a thing of dreams and not an option for me. The fact that a low-level job cannot make me rich. The fact that my goal and aspirations are to be a leader. The fact that my dad was a politician, and I aspire to be one too. The fact that my creativity may afford me all the riches this life can afford me. The choice of being rich or poor, of being who I am, of knowing what I want. My only choice is to be an entrepreneur, knowing that while I was on probation, I couldn't get a good job. Entrepreneurs are usually rich. That's my choice. I want to be rich, and I can be as a result of America and its former and current leaders.

To Be

To be that individual others dream of is what every person should desire. That is my desire: to be Skip Flanagan. To be whoever and whatever I want to be, not what others want me to be.

I have learned some very precious lessons. I am human, and like any other citizen, I sometimes wonder. I must wonder as a result of the injustices that have been directed toward people of my same skin shade. I have to look at the word *racism*. I have to look at the word *discrimination*. I have to consider the word *conspiracy*, and *global conspiracy*. Therefore, I have to consider the forces that I have no knowledge of, the hidden hand. I have to think of the spirituality of this life, considering a higher power. As with history, it will repeat itself. Things that happened in the past will repeat themselves again. So let's look at a bigger book of prophecy.

From my readings, I can now easily see how the great holocaust is about to be carried out as we approach the year 2000. I can now see how there will be global destruction and rebellion. I guess it's kind of easy to turn the cheek to these realities when pleasure can be achieved by so many other means. The most beautiful of horses are sometimes destroyed, and this trend will continue. I guess we can only be caught up in this hell. Yet one must understand the recyclability of the human inner spirit. What this means is just as we exist here today, so we will exist in this galaxy once again. Death is the magic that I speak of in my other book, *I Dreamed You, a Legend!* The spirit as it exists in you now will recreate itself somewhere else, in some other material wonderland. This is where you will receive penalties for your sins. This is the hell that the Bible and many historians speak of.

I try to tie in my experiences in this life. In the midst, you search for some discipline. How can I rightfully assume my place in this hellish society? What kind of heaven can I enjoy on this earth full of discrimination, crime, and cancer? When you look at the numbers, I'm the minority. When you look at the social programs, I'm the recipient of most or all the funds allotted for these programs. Thus, how can I realistically have a chance to succeed in this great country? Who can I be?

I must first disassociate myself with these types of associations. I must pretend that these conditions don't exist. I must get rid of group thinking and use reverse psychology, by turning this bad into a good. My thoughts are, "Get this car going in the right direction!" I must succeed no matter what the cost, because I have to be a leader for my kids. True, I can get a job, and my kids can get jobs. Still, why can't I be rich? I must have the disposition of Job. I must pursue goals in the manner that Jesus did. I will return as Jesus did, returning to claim my place in history as a representation of all the persecuted. I will stand strong as a shining example of all the freedom fighters and everyday people who died as a result of this conspiracy and holocaust. We must fight until justice is won! This can be done simply by participating in the political process and not giving up on the American dream. This dream includes all Americans.

A selective process to individually associate with those individuals the deeds, actions, and injustices that are their own will be used as a basis for the implementation of punishment for past sins, thereby enabling the appropriate punishment to be enforced against these villains who oppose peace and equality. During a time where richness is measured in terms of the number of materials a person owns, and where power is an excuse to defy biblical principles, what can I be? I choose to be a servant to God. To be patient. To be tortured and persecuted for wanting to be. To be me. To be me is not supposed to be good. To be me, given the odds to be me, is something many of you (whether educated or uneducated) could not be.

Rich

Rich means the unlimited access to materials and the money necessary to purchase these materials. I guess it's having one million dollars, one might say. You can buy a house. You can buy your dream car and still have a lot of money left over to spend. You are also afforded the ability to look very rich. You can buy clothes and maybe even buy love.

As I put love to its greatest test, I can see why the craving for money and riches is so great. As I ride in my black truck with the hood dented up and the lawnmowers on back, I can easily be persuaded in some other totally different type of occupation. You see, I'm a dreamer. I dream of the riches and of a dream spouse. I dream of one day being rich. Nevertheless, I don't let my dreams and ambitions to become rich cloud my means by which I will attempt to get there.

Illegally, I could get rich real quick. I could get the big car, big house, and a beautiful spouse too. The money is everything, and they don't care. If you can take care of them, it's all good. You can get a spouse with the money. This was one of the harder lessons to learn. I never would have imagined that so many would sell their souls for the love of money. I observe the manner in which so many choose to sell their souls to the devil. I further understand that everyone doesn't worship God as I do. I think it's every God-fearing man's desire to see every other person in fear of this same God, in alliance with this same God. Shockingly, to the contrary there are millions who worship the devil, and they worship as diligently as we worship God. The devil has access to the same materials that are at God's disposal, but only if it is God's will, of course.

What is rich? Rich to me is the accumulation of wealth over a long period of time. To some fellows, it's the ability to pay a car note and drive a fancy car down the boulevard. In short, it's having the car title but not the capital necessary to sustain this type of lifestyle. Rich to me would be having about four or five million put up, and a daily income of about ten thousand. Lucrative CDs and other investments, college savings for my kids, and liquid assets with a million or more net worth. The ability to travel in a private jet or a private yacht. Being in love and having all your bills paid for, because love and no money results in knocks on the door. There is a company called Rent by Me. "Hey, we come to pick up that stereo system. Oh, yeah, and that sofa. Go ahead and put the microwave on that loveseat. Put that beeper right here next to mine, and that jewelry round your neck. Here is your VCR tape. *JFK*? Oh, that was a good movie."

Rich would be having a nice home, but not necessarily that big. I have kids, but I'm single; they'll come by on occasion. Furthermore, I've been on this struggle by myself, so I may as well go alone. On my deed, Mr. Skip Flanagan could have a pool outside. In the bottom of the pool in cursive letters is "Skip Flanagan" made in diamonds. Here comes G-roots the St. Bernard, and B-Gee the girl.

Rich would also be taking a day off to go to LA to visit Ced and Ronnie. Halle and I could meet in LA while I'm visiting the Bill Maher show. I would invite her to Houston to relax at my newly purchased suite. Meanwhile, I'm listening to a nice R&B CD—maybe some Aaron Hall, Kirk Whalum, or Brian McKnight—in a high0rise building. Of course, I'm on the floor next to the top with glass across the whole side of the room. I open the curtains and tie a rope around them. It's about 3:00 in the morning. I look outside, and it's a full moon. A bird passes by the moon. What a beautiful sight. The stars are out. "Look … that's a falling star. Right there." Halle turns around while I look down, viewing the city lights. The light is green with few cars on the scene; I guess these are the guys who have just come home from the club. I excitedly walk toward the sofa while admiring the structure of the room: woodgrain walls, arched walkways.

I tread toward this sectional sofa, a burgundy leather beaded piece, and assume my spot on it. Of course it's next to Halle, as she sits with her legs crossed with matching negligee. A chilled, ice-cooled, trophy-like vase sits in front of us. The Don Perignon is chilled. Two glasses sit next to the vase. I pour her a drink then pour mine. We both sit back as I grab the remote and turn up the music. I grab the remote and change the channel to a video on BET. It was a video by Howard Hewitt, "Show Me." Nice song. I'm smelling like soap and Claiborne for men. "Aah." I sit back and relax. Next, I click to the Made CD by Skip Flanagan.

"Wait—somebody is knocking." I get up and answer the door. It's the flower guy. I invite him in, and all two hundred flowers. I told him to place them in front of the sixty-two-inch flat-screen. One can see the equalizer going up in the system that is built into the wall. He finishes. *Knock, knock.* Oh it's the banner guy. I had a banner made that says, "I love you, Halle!" I told him to tie it in front, across the flowers. I reach for my pockets but don't have any money. I asked Halle for some money. She asks me how much do I need. I explain, "About two hundred dollars." I tip the guys one hundred dollars apiece. They're looking at my gal, so I usher them out the door. I walked to my room, retrieve about a thousand dollars, and give it to Halle. She reasons, "You don't have to."

I insist. "Take it, baby. This is a very special night for me."

I further explain that it would totally ruin the moment if she didn't accept the money. She does. We sit. She embraces me. I reach for my drink while gazing at her. So beautiful, so sexy. Inside I smile because my heart is ill-equipped to handle this sudden rush of emotions. I try to keep my composure, being at a point where I feel very comfortable with who I am and how far I've come. My greatest challenge is to get into her mind and convey how much I dig her, telling her that I'm deeply in love with her. I must show her that this moment is definitely special, expressing that this is something I would only do for her. I nervously ponder what she might be thinking. With her uncompromising beauty, she has action at any living human being. The relentless thirst for her has to be great around the world, shared by many men as well as many WNBA players. I'm in tough competition.

I briskly cut the idle chatter and reach into my pocket. I pull out the biggest diamond that can comfortably fit on a ring finger without interfering with the basics of reading a script or any household duties. I hand her the diamond, covered gently by a white cotton cloth. She unfolds the cloth and then gazes at the diamond. Her eyes gaze at the diamond with a look of sincere appreciation—that woman's look. The affection is overflowing, and this moment is second to none in my life. This room is ill-equipped to handle the constant overflow of emotions present. I calmly yet anxiously get up and lead her to the room, strutting through the arched doors. We hug as we walk together.

She wants to get into the Jacuzzi. I head toward the bed. It is an enormous bed, pure wood, with large poles and white satin pillow slips. On the sides of the bed are white mink floor mats. I lie down in the bed and turn the CD player to Tony! Toni! Toné! I pull the sheet to my chest, allowing the gold medallion to hang over the white satin sheets, and take Halle into view. She smiles and asks me to come join her. While enjoying the salacious atmosphere, I take a sip from my glass with a canyon-wide smile.

I place the glass on the marble table with gold trim next to the bed, underneath the silk glass cloth. I flip back the satin sheets. *Da Crime Family* comes on. "Someday the light will shine on this ghetto of mine!" My head nods a couple of times, signifying agreement. I move toward the Jacuzzi. With only my silk boxers on, I get in. She smiles and grabs my medallion. She observes it and then asks, "What is eighty-one hundred?" I kept smiling and jamming. My sweetheart looks at me intensely. I'm not shy, so I look back. Now the Isley Brothers are on: "You'll never ever walk alone!" I grab her hands and pull her close. We kiss, then I show her to the satin sheets, the Isley Brothers still playing.

We wake up the next morning to Stevie Wonder's "These Three Words." It's time for her to leave. She's scheduled to be in Hollywood at 10:00 a.m. Someone is knocking at the door. I answer. It's the housekeeper. She brings in my clothes from the cleaners, Skip Flanagan Apparel. She brings in Halle's clothes,

Halle Flanagan Apparel. We get dressed. Halle is dressed in a blue satin dress with dark blue shoes, and she has on a blue mink coat. I have on Skip Flanagan shoes (blue), Skip Flanagan belt (gold buckle and black), and blue pleated Skip Flanagan slacks. I have a white silk shirt with buttons and a half collar. There is also a dark blue mink jacket. Diamond ring. Brand-new haircut. Medallion. Watch. Hand pouch with a thousand dollars. We pace down the hall holding hands and get on the elevator. I intimately caress her and tell her how much I love her before we got off at the ground floor.

As we walk toward the car, I push the button on the remote so the doors unlock, and to idle the motor. When I open her door, the music playing is Lil' Keke's "Good Part." I close her door and then get in the driver's seat. Once inside, I adjust the AC to seventy degrees°. I select number one again on the CD player, refusing to miss anything. Next, I turn on the screens. While pulling out, the lady on the Rolls Royce pops up. My license plates reads "WAT NEX" as I hit the strip. I have bulletproof windows. I'm jammin'. I'm rich.

Success Is a Given

Dreams are fascinating. You can sit down and think of something so wonderful, something so divine. Then the truth sets in. The realities of life. The bills. The existing problems. This world.

It's hard for me to believe that in other countries, the laws are nonexistent, and killing is a sport. I wonder what would have happened if I were born in Egypt or something. What would my options for success be?

In America, the accumulation of wealth is the standard for success. How much money you have. How many cars you have. How many homes you have. There is a scale for success. Success is measurable by multiples of hundreds. Multiples of thousands. Multiples of millions. I guess I try to accumulate this type of wealth for these very reasons. I guess this is why I fail, because I'm caught up in this madness! Once again, I see light at the end of the tunnel. I am physically capable of doing lots of things on this earth. I am this talented individual who lacks only opportunity. To me, success is a given. I look at my success as just a couple of years away, wholeheartedly hoping that I'm prepared for it, hoping that I'm ready to be Skip Flanagan.

There's no reason to believe that I cannot be successful, no reason to believe that I will fail. I control my destiny. I live in America, and the sky is definitely the limit. I now see how the accumulation of wealth has become relatively easy, enabling me to take control of my destiny. I have all the respect in the world now for the American system. I love America! Thanks, Americans.

I like to talk about the three things that I believe can help any US citizen. Those things are education, specialization, and creation. Education should be foremost in your attempts to progress in this world, no matter who you are. Regardless of what color you are, success is an option for you. Your education should include elementary, middle school, and high school. This will allow you to have a knowledge base and a frame of reference for real life, or for higher learning at college. College is where you specialize in a trade or field of study. This is more difficult learning. Once you have finished your studying, you are then labeled a professional. Your service and your knowledge demand compensation. Remember, you are a professional. Therefore, you know a lot about your particular field of study. This is a reward for your studying, a reward for your diligence and patience. If your professionalism doesn't land you a job, then it's up to you to create your own job. You must now become an entrepreneur.

Life can be difficult. You simply have to keep on trying. Success is the gift to the overachiever. Yet all these options are at your disposal due to the fact that you're an American. Success is just that simple. Even so, you still have to be creative and do the things to ensure that will make you successful. Work is a lifelong process. Learning will take place for the remainder of your life. Ups and downs are a part of this life. Struggle is a part of this life. Strength and patience are all a part of this life.

God should be primary in everyone's life. He is the key to fending off misfortunes and those things that seem like bad luck. He can make this process much easier. After having a taste of success so many times in my life, I can only encourage others to do things that I feel will bring joy to their lives. Success for me is completing all my dreams. Success for me is being that guy that I see I am. Success for me is being Skip Flanagan. Entrepreneur. Writer. Minister. Politician. Film writer. Given my disposition and my faith in God, I can see all these things. Success isn't something that you luck up on. Success is not something that you stumble on. Success isn't something that you win in the lottery. Success is pursued. Success is earned. Yeah, with education, specialization, or creation. Yeah, success is inevitable. Yes, success is a given!

Understanding the Terms and Conditions

If I'm a citizen in America, I know that there are certain levels of success, consequences of failure, and benefits of getting a college education. There are benefits of becoming a police officer, along with the dangers of being a police officer. I understand where education can lead me and where working can lead to. I realize there are problems as well as solutions. I acknowledge that there are racist groups, militants in America, and individuals who hate America.

Do you know? Do you know the terms and conditions of this life? Do you know the terms and conditions of this world? Do you know what it takes to succeed in America? The terms that one must know about are simple. Either you succeed or you fail. You win or you lose. You fall. You get up. You cry. You hustle. You scratch. You get up. You don't quit. You run. You hide. You pray. You live. You learn. You change. You understand more as you live. You remain loyal. You say thanks. You have class. You have dignity. You tell them you are American! That means you are a winner.

As a kid, you live as a kid. You understand that you're a kid, and you live as such. You take advantage of the moments that you are a kid because these moments will be no more. You play. You hurt yourself. You tell your mom. You look forward to Christmas. You look forward to all the holidays. You are a kid. You watch the cartoons. You play as a kid would. You respect Mom. You respect your elders. You say, "Yes, sir." You say, "Yes, ma'am." You are a kid. A good kid. You excel in school. You don't worry about the problems because those are not your problems. You are a kid. You have no means to solve those problems. Yet by going to school and getting your education, you can make sure that these are problems that you don't run into down the line. You plan to finish your education.

As a young adult, you have to concentrate on getting an education or securing a job. You have to start planning your life. You have to start positioning yourself to be successful. Position yourself to take care of your family. You do plan on having a family, don't you? You are human? Yeah. You have to pay your own bills. You're going to have babies. You're going to have to live this real life. As a kid and as a young adult, everything seems relatively easy. You're excited about becoming an adult. You're excited about being able to drive, being able to use four letter words. You're excited about life and all that it has in store for you. Now, here comes the real world. You hope that you are prepared. You hope that you have enough education. You hope that you are who you say you are.

What are your options in this life? To survive. To put food on the table. To be happy. To be American. What is being American? An American is one who is cognizant of one's own heritage and family background. One who understands the history of America. One who understands the diversity that exists in America. One who respects this diversity. One who respects other US citizens. One who has access to all parts of the American dream.

The American dream being to fulfill all one's dreams and one's potential. That dream also is owning property and the unabated right to pursue happiness. Easier said than done. So what are the conditions? In this world, there are problems. Cancer, crime, discrimination, and racism are just a few of the problems that you will have to face in the real world. With that in mind, you have to find out how to participate in making this America and this government work for you. You have to see where you fit in and what things you can change, ensuring that those things are for the good all countrymen. We're in a time where we're still attempting to make this a peaceful coexistence. We're going to work this thing out no matter the terms or the conditions, as Americans, as examples for the rest of the world. We are the best. Just look around you.

Entrepreneur or Consumer; Democrat vs. Republican

I guess everyone is that word, schizophrenic. Oh, I'm just crazy. I'm just a this or that type of dude. Yet certain situations justify my thinking. So let's take a look at how we, that type of people, think. While growing up in Third Ward, I knew about food stamps and government assistance. I knew how it felt to be poor. My mom worked sunup to sundown, changing jobs here and there. Yet we had the best clothes and went to all the places that the rich kids went. Therefore, I guess we weren't real ghetto kids. We were just in the area.

We moved to South Park, which was a little bit better than Third Ward, and bought a home. The American dream was within our reach. Still, money didn't come as fast as it should. This made us Democrats. From my perspective, a Democrat was one who believed in diversity and helping the poor. To my belief, all Blacks were Democrats and all Whites were Republicans. So what could we do if a Republican got elected? Nothing, I guess.

To my belief, a Republican was one who was rich and worried only about taxes. All these things are not true. When I saw a Black Republican, I would automatically say to myself, "Uncle Tom." I didn't feel that a Black guy had a justifiable reason to be a Republican. Moreover, they could never be friends of mine. It's 2011; I've accomplished a lot so far and am positioned to be rich. I'm pondering politics, thinking about one day running for city council, and considering my agenda as a politician. It would be a universal platform and agenda, not smothering out the major problems that exist in the urban community.

Crime, AIDS, schools, parks, streets—these are problems that would be priority to me. A universal Republican platform may not cover these areas. However, as a rich man, I would be at odds with whether to be Republican or Democrat. I could definitely be a Republican due to the fact that some things that are a part of their platform may affect my well-being. Some of the things that are a part of their agenda may affect my business. So which party should I side with? Selfishly, I could be a Republican. Nonetheless, as a part of a group, it would probably be best that I be a Democrat.

I thought about how individuals who worked for someone would be better off being Democrat. The worker or the consumer. The employee. The one who works for the Republican, the entrepreneur. The Democrat or the consumer is more concerned with restricting the rights of the Republican entrepreneur. Minimum wage. Let's take a look at minimum wage. I'm an entrepreneur who is a Democrat for now, I guess due more to the diversity and change issue than anything else. I have the utmost respect for Jimmy Carter, Harry Truman, Thomas Jefferson, and Bill Clinton. These are individuals who had more on their agendas than dollars and cents. They had a vision of a perfect America in mind and in heart. They were in search of peace. How could this peace be achieved? By soothing the hurt of African Americans and assisting them in becoming part of American society. Economics play a major role in this process. When you look at living, higher education, and ridding the inner cities of social problems, then you see the importance of having an elected official with these issues at heart.

I remember when Bill Clinton was elected, America was receptive to change. I sensed a greater sense of urgency in White Americans. I could see how badly they wanted change and also peace. Every God-fearing compatriot was receptive to this change. Bill Clinton's presidential inauguration and presidency should go down in history as one of the greatest miracles in the twentieth century. This was definitely a great show of diversity throughout its duration. In 1999 during Al Gore's presidential bid, he tried to distance himself from Bill Clinton. I believe that distancing himself from Bill Clinton was a big mistake. To do so was a big betrayal and showed disloyalty to someone who made it possible for him to be in the position to run for president.

Today, we have to consider which party is best for America.

When I looked at the elections, at that time I liked Bill Bradley, a former athlete. I believed that he would have made a good president. George W. Bush was also a candidate at the time. George Bush was truly a leader. I was raised in Houston and was a Texas native, so I knew a lot about President Bush. George Bush has never been one to sit back and wait for someone to tell him what to do. He was a strict politician with a tough-guy image. He is real religious, and his platform always included the poor and minority concerns. I was watching television and saw President Bush kiss a little black girl. I believed in the sincerity of all his moves. I believed then that George Bush was going to be the next president. He did become the president of the United States of America.

As an entrepreneur, I'm constantly challenged to come up with new, innovative ideas—something that comes rather easily to me. I don't even mind sharing the wealth. Nevertheless, wealth and the accumulation of this wealth is one of the most difficult tasks at one's disposal. Having to come up with the idea is already somewhat difficult. Then fending off the corruption and hungry non-entrepreneurs (leeches) is a difficult task. My lessons as an entrepreneur have further shown me that the very things that can establish your success can also contribute to your failure. I proceed with nothing to lose. Life's problems and injustices justify my writing and my thinking as a die-hard entrepreneur.

Me, an individual who possesses full knowledge of what is necessary to succeed, a legal entrepreneur, unable to get a small business loan, unable to get any form of assistance to help facilitate my success. That leaves me basically doomed. Me, this hardworking man. My struggle not being pretty, now I must have vast wealth in order to even date. My job title is a prerequisite to dating. My vehicle is also a prerequisite. My place of residence is a prerequisite. In essence, me chasing the American dream is wrong. In contrast, for those that have already eclipsed this level of success, it's OK. I have a certain way that I have to be now. Truth and real life are hard realities.

The truth is I will continue to struggle until I get a significant financial boost. To me, this financial boost will be a result of my creativity and a tribute to my struggle. The lessons I learned. The real America. Untapped. Positioning myself not solely on this new hobby. Strategically, using a good to facilitate and stimulate my success as a US citizen. I'm proud of the fact, and it's still a fact that so many individuals don't understand. Still having to justify my talents. Just read: not only is this good writing, but it's some of the best writing that will ever be revealed to the public eye. Justifying my talents and my place in the sun—something that will be a difficult challenge. In the middle of trying to solve all the problems that will make this a perfect scenario, I must do this. I must come up with some of the greatest ideas, even though I stated in my first book that I wanted to be a part of the peace process directly and indirectly. I noticed an article in a news circulation in my city. It stated unity is not racism. I stated unity is not supremacy. Now, am I that word or what? I'm a child of God. This is why I keep him front and center, at the beginning and the end of my hierarchy.

My truths to forever be doubted. I just ask that the individuals who doubt go and research prove me wrong, because via pictures and via verbal exchange, the truth will forever be evident as it can't be hidden. Most definitely it is not from God. I can't do anything about conspiracy; I'm not that powerful. As a matter of fact, I'm not that powerful at all. However, in comparison to some of the greater writers of this time, match me up with anyone. Hand my book to one who likes to read. Then ask that person which one was the better of the two. Simple truth.

I'm a little giving in praise and other exaggerations in my efforts to promote certain things, but when it comes to actual occurrences and events, the truth is front and center. I guess the same truths that once destroyed me are now the same truths that those very individuals cannot take. I accepted the consequences then, and I accept them now. Who is that word now? *I Dreamed You, a Legend* will forever be one of the greatest writings of all time. Times preserved by pictures, forever to be able to show the entrepreneur in me. Forever to show the patriotism in me from beginning to end. Forever being able to show the roadmap to peace, and forever to have a shadow of doubt to the authenticity of the work and this writer's intentions. Believe every single word, because they are all my thinking and are all true.

Monetarily and materially, with those associations I could never win. News flash: with me and God, I can win. I can win as an entrepreneur and have good judgment as a Republican, because to be placed in such a situation will have been the result of some very creative men. Meanwhile, when spending and placed in the position of the consumer, I must then do those things that are mutually beneficial to me. For this entrepreneur, this exchange must be a pleasant one. A friendly one. A business one. As a great businessman, I can only wait, because I've entrusted my talents in someone else, knowing fully what I've done as trust is now involved in this process. I believe.

Even though an entrepreneur is described in your business journal as a risk taker, this is a mild risk considering what is to be lost and the possibilities of what can be gained. But if we look at it materially, we will miss. If we look at this spiritually, I've done some of the best and most effective, spiritually rewarding writing of this time. I have crossed and will cross all walks of life, touch hearts near and afar. Unfortunately, the realization that those consumers who are around me will miss is something I must accept.

Only I can see me, this great writer. The manifestation of this prophecy is so hard for others to accept. This miracle is that they will forever not be able to see, because their minds are too small to see the manner in which God works. Me, this humble servant, simply suffering as would any normal citizen. Having full knowledge that there are many out there just like me. The best is yet to come. Their hearts will be eased of the pain and psychological ills that have plagued them for so many years. During these days of judgement, during these days of true distinction, where the truth is now very distinguishable from falsehood. The truth is that this entrepreneur who now must position himself to help many consumers who want to become entrepreneurs. I have the choice to do so. Their choice is now being easier, because I have paved the pathway for such a thing to happen. Choice and consequences are important in this life. Freedom is also important in this life. The Ten Commandments are important in this life. The Bible and holy Koran are important in this life. Discipline is important in this life. Consistency is important in this life. Me being true to myself is most important in this life outside of God. Me having the choice as a result of being American, the option of being a Democrat or a Republican. Me having the choice to be an entrepreneur or a consumer. Granted, I also have to think about the danger of such choices, and therefore I think about whether it is best for myself and my family. This world keeps me as that word. Or am I? Republican or Democrat? Entrepreneur or consumer?

What a life. Times have changed dramatically. America elected a Black president. His name is Barack Obama. Barack Obama is a Democrat. The election of Barack Obama was historic. Barack Obama being elected for president was a relief for all Americans. This election signaled a new day in America.

The world watched as America got past a major psychological obstacle. That obstacle was racism. This was confirmation that America had changed. Nation after nation watched as Barack Obama changed perceptions around the world. People were crying. People were holding hands. This was a day to remember. I recall hearing people hollering for blocks at a time. People were screaming. On this night, there was a peace like never before. The change that Barack Obama claimed he represented was here.

When I saw the events, I could only smile. I could only share in the joy of so many people from around the world. The election of Barack Obama was a day I never thought I would see. I had always questioned America's willingness to release the reins of power to a black man. My doubts have been high for years. Yet I always held out hope that things would change. Things have changed.

President Obama has done a lot of things. A lot of the things he has done, I don't agree with. His support of same-sex unions, his support of the abolition of the "Don't ask, don't tell" military policy. The mandate that Americans must have health insurance. He has yet to discuss problems in urban communities. He has yet to address the crime in urban neighborhoods.

President Obama has more of a Republican platform than a Democratic one. He bailed out Big Business and banks. He loaned money to Big Business. He gave bonuses to the wealthy executives. Yet he insisted that most Americans are lazy. Wow!

If the big businesses need help, so do the small businesses. He has yet to give a stimulus check to the American people. He is a different type of president.

When George Bush was in office, the earned income credit increased dramatically. He handed out lots of money to churches so that they could create programs to help the community. He donated lots of money to Black colleges. He gave out stimulus checks during the year. He brought in Rod Paige, an African American educator, and Rod Paige created No Child Left Behind. A lot of people say that it was a failure. They argue about the usefulness of such a program. Yet the original premise of this program was great. The implementation of it by educators around the country? Now, that's another story. The premise of the program alone says a lot.

President George Bush had a very diverse White House. Collin Powell, Condoleezza Rice, Kirbyjon Caldwell, and so many more. I'm trying to think of a notable African American in the Barack Obama cabinet. Huh?

I use these facts to show how color does not mean as much as one's actions. I believe a lot of African Americans support President Obama solely based on color.

That's not to say President Obama is not a good president. I just don't believe he is a great president. It is my belief that African Americans have to be more versatile and more active in politics and those decisions that affect their day-to-day lives. I believe that African Americans have to go through the whole political process before choosing the candidate of choice and voting.

I further believe that we have to step outside the Democratic Party and consider the Republican Party. I believe that a lot of African Americans automatically assume that they are Democrats at birth, and they have to remain Democrats until they die. Not so! Once again, the Republican Party is supposed to be for the rich, and the Democratic Party is supposed to represent the poor. That being true, why would you automatically label yourself inferior and label yourself a Democrat without even researching? What does the Democratic Party represent? Do I need food stamps? Will I always be a consumer?

These are questions that individuals must ask themselves. Which party is best for you? If I own my business and need tax breaks, is it OK if I look out for myself by becoming a Republican? Why do I have to be a Democrat? What is the end goal of the Democratic Party?

I say these things because I believe it is time we look out for our own self-interest. If we are going to be a unified America and not a polarized America, we have to look at legislation through a good or bad lens and not a black-and-white lens. Individual families in America have to vote for the candidates that can best help their situation. You don't go in the booth and press all Democrat. We have to do better than that. It is time to move forward as a people and as a country. I believe that for the children of America and for the sake of the country, the thinking has to change. I believe more work and detail has to be put into who we are and what we want to become. There are so many careers that need names on them. We have to focus on careers, and those careers will lead to business opportunities. You can be whatever you want to be. You can be a doctor, lawyer, or scientist. You can be a Republican. You simply have to free yourself and your thinking. You are a person of many hats. It's your decision which one you wear.

If I Were President

If I were the president, I'm not sure how I would feel. I really don't think it would be something that I would like. The way politics are played in America, I don't believe this is something that would be high on my agenda. Yet being president of the United States of America would be a great accomplishment.

When I think about presidents, I think about John F. Kennedy, Jimmy Carter, and Bill Clinton. I think of them because I consider them great presidents. When I think of them, I think of diversity. I think of people who tried to bring all Americans together. These were presidents with moral and spiritual obligations. I believe that a great president has to have a futuristic vision of and for America. He or she has to be able to envision America at least ten years into the future.

When I think of America, I think of a country that's a big melting pot. I think of a country with many different races of people. A complex nation. A nation that needs a great leader. A leader that can balance the needs of all Americans.

When I look at these presidents, I recall them wanting to do things to help the poor. When I think about the problems in America, I think about urban neighborhoods and crime. I think about the small businesses that have disappeared. I think about the moral decline. I think about the new culture. I attempt to envision the new culture.

When I think about presidents, I think of which ones attempted to solve the problems of urban neighborhoods. Once again I must say George Bush put the money where the people in the urban neighborhoods could get it. A ten-thousand-dollar income tax return is a lot of money. If you are smart, this is equivalent to a small business loan. John F. Kennedy did some great things. He was good at putting the vision out there and holding people accountable. He held your foot to the fire until the task was completed. He got a lot done. Bill Clinton can be credited with bringing America together. He had a "tough on crime" legacy. Three strikes, and you are out. He was a true diplomat. Jimmy Carter is always the first on the scene when it comes to injustices. I have a lot of respect for Jimmy Carter.

You can't turn your back to the real problems and expect the people not to see and feel the neglect. Neighborhoods are dangerous. You have to leave your doors locked, and your pistols have to stay cocked. Living in urban neighborhoods is like living in a prison. It's unsafe to travel or go to gas stations. Everyone's life is in danger right now. Yet nobody is complaining or saying anything about the crime and the things that are going on. Either they are blind or they don't care.

If I were president, I would first address the crime in urban neighborhoods. First-offense violent criminals would not be eligible for probation. I would reduce the cost of traffic violations and make them affordable. I would make surcharges payable for one year only. I would make child support a decision between married couples. I would make the first child eligible for child support in nonmarried couples. Females who have never been married would have to consult the father, and a court date would be established. At the court proceedings, the father would have the right to custody if he could establish the ability to take care of the child. The act of filing child support is equivalent with abandonment, and therefore the other spouse is automatically granted full custody. Child support would no longer be a "get rich" scheme.

I would make the death penalty legal and standard around the country. We would execute prisoners within two years after establishing guilt. Any probationer or parolee would have to attend at least one viewing of a criminal put to death.

I would reduce the median home prices and create a negotiable wage law where employers can negotiate a rate of pay for employers that may be lower than minimum wage. If the employee agrees to it, then you pay it! I would limit lawsuits and hold media and magazines accountable for printing private business. Malicious stories would be eligible for fines up to one million dollars.

I would give big businesses tax breaks if they paid the salary for at least one employee of a business that it partners with, or a business that produces goods for that business, or any business that has a common interest with the big business. I would make grants easily accessible and create legislation that would stimulate small businesses. I would encourage males to go into teaching and education. I would reimplement prayer in school and the recital of the Pledge of Allegiance.

I would declare the United States a Christian nation. I would evaluate all legislation and discard all useless legislation that I feel causes undue burdens.

If I were president, I would fix America and the world!

Kings and Queens

I guess I ought to take it easy on the females. Just like everything else. If there weren't any problems, then I wouldn't have said anything. There are problems with relationships. Just listen. People say, "I ain't going out. Ain't no telling what's out there." "You have to stick with one partner these days." All the while, they're steady clubbin', steady "bleeping," as soon as the songs come on. What we got to do? Now we have more obstacles in the way as we try to find a queen or king. All those diversions kicked patience dead in the ass! You gotta grab one quick. Hold on. Pray. Hope she is the right one.

I know women are going to argue, "Those dudes don't want to work!" I feel you, and I've been saying this the whole while. They say I've been too negative. I'm talking about our people. No. I'm trying to show them what is going on. First-class life: this is what I want. This is what you want. The best cars. The best houses. The best women. The best jobs. The best of this ghetto world. The best of the real world.

How can you get it? The right way. The legal way. That's the only way to last long. I've been around long enough to see a lot of different things. I've been around long enough to see people come and go. I've been around long enough to see tragedies happen. Innocent people die. Good people die. Christians die. Muslims die. Rich people die. Kings die. Queens die.

Life is much easier now. I have to look at this life in a different light. I have to look at it in terms of God the Almighty. So many people have died over millions of years. I wonder sometimes, *Where do they go? What's next? Heaven or hell? What's next after life on Earth?* To me, it's simple. You see Moses. You see Jesus. You can imagine their struggles. Someone who brought the good news and happy to be of God, only to be persecuted for bringing something that could bring happiness to the masses. I now see my destiny in the same light. I now must strengthen my relationship with Jesus even more. Knowing even more now. Understanding the need for such a person. Being able to see why he died such a tragic death. Jesus, a King. I must strive to be Jesus-like. Not a bad role model. Not a bad example for someone who loves and respects God. I love Jesus! I must never allow anyone to sway me from my beliefs. I must be smart enough to know why the world loves him so. Jesus was the Messiah. Jesus encompassed the teachings of all the prophets before him. He also laid the foundation for the prophets to come after him. You feel me?

God has time. He can wait as long as you can. If you are impatient, you can meet him today or tomorrow. It's up to you. I'll just wait. No, God, I'm in no hurry. I can wait. Take him. I'm still working. Still doing your work. Still suffering. Still positioning myself to do greater works. I just hope I'll be around to see the fruits of my harvest and have a little fun. I hope this wasn't all work related. Give me time to spend with my queen, to give her all the love I can give. Hopefully, I will receive that love back. See, I keep hoping. I keep praying. I stay on my knees.

God stays in my thoughts. God stays in my heart. Every second. Every minute. Every hour. Every day. Every night. Every week. Every month. Every quarter. Every year. I need him. I didn't create cups, fruit, or this universe. I didn't create steel that can be used to make cars. I didn't create mathematics. I didn't create breath. I didn't create sound. Who did? Not you. You're a man. I didn't create atoms. I didn't create the evening.

I was watching *Jerry Springer* one day, and a guy said, "God created Adam and Eve, not Adam and Steve." Of course, he was referring to homosexuality. I remember in college, I did a paper on homosexuality. I did my research, and my findings were interesting. There are some individuals who are really born homosexual. One guy said, "I knew at about four years old." I had to believe him. I was like, *Damn! I believe him.* I believe in this theory. I respect the homosexual's position. I respect the fact that he is gay. However, what I don't like about homosexuals is the fact that they don't respect your position on that. They think everyone should be gay because they're gay. I say, "Man, get your ass down the way with that bullshit!" Just like somebody reading this. Oh, yeah, "He gay." He wouldn't have written this. No way, buddy. No way, Steve. Where did you come from?

Most gay people like straight people. If you're gay, you need to quit trying to convert straight folk. It's like buying a Firestone tire and having the *t* missing. You cannot sell that tire. You put it with the others that have those letters missing. You feel me? It's like, if I'm in a Diet Coke factory, and I put too much diet in it, it has a bad taste. Those cans are going to be put aside, put together. No disrespect. It's time we accept the facts. You are gay? Fine. You stay gay. Gay goes with gay, not straight. This is where they're going to talk about choice.

You see, in life there is a hierarchy. There are rules and laws. There are things we can and can't do. If I see a cliff, I know I'm physically capable of jumping off that cliff. That fact is understood. If I had a pistol, I know that I could shoot and kill myself. These are options. Yet these are things that are against God's order. There is punishment for sin. We as US citizens are spoiled. We assume that the things we are not supposed to do are OK as long as we don't get caught, but that is not the case. Breaking the law is breaking the law. Sin is sin. There are consequences for both.

We as humans don't know what death is, so we flirt with the possibility. We take chances—bad chances. It's like telling people not to smoke cocaine. They've seen the effects of smoking cocaine. They see the dopeheads. They see the addicts. In spite of that, they say, "Ah, I can handle it." I guess that's that super X chromosome in them. They try the cocaine. Then that super X turns into a small Y, or the big "Why me?" Fool, you know. History has shown that the majority of people who smoke cocaine become addicted. What makes you different? The same rules apply with homosexuality. Some know it's wrong, so they say, "I don't know what's wrong with these men these days. They don't know how to treat a woman." They use this as a reason to try Madam instead of Adam. Now they like women.

Whatever happened to patience? Remember earlier, I told you we totally kicked patience in the ass. The world was supposed to end in the year 2000. The Bible talks about homosexuality. People use clichés that reference homosexuality to their advantage. I'll be damned. So straight women can now be seen with gay women, faking like they are gay. Faking like they don't want anything to do with men. A gay female is just a female assuming the role of a man. The lady now says, "She knows how to make me feel good. She knows what spots get me hot." I'm like, damn. That's all you had to do: tell me, girl. My mission is to please you. You know what I mean? I love you, girl! What? I'm like Keith Sweat. What is the deal? Let me know, baby. I can put the Johnny Gill or the Aaron Hall in, and it's action. You tell me what to do in the bed. Hey, it's on!

Thus, they continue to experiment only because they can. Only because it's not against the law. Only because there are no known consequences for their actions. Wait until they get those secret indictments, God's indictments. You feel me? Experimentation is all it is. Just like cocaine, they get used to it, get comfortable with it. Don't want to stop doing it. Don't think it ought to be any downside to a relationship. Don't think there are supposed to be any problems. You feel me? Everything is not going to be lovey-dovey. Life is not always that way, so we have to ride out the problem. You have to be in it for the duration, till death do you part.

God has to be present in the relationship. Order. A hierarchy. I have a hierarchy. I have dreams for myself, set goals for myself, and have a standard by which I live. I heard about my grandfather, and he was a great man. I must continue his works. My dad was also a great man, so I must continue his legacy. I believe in God. I must do his will and live my life to a high standard. I must live as a great man would, as other great ones have done before me.

Kings were rewarded with riches in times of old. They had thrones, cities named after them. Some people worshipped the kings. I've never seen a king in this country. I have yet to see royalty, so for myself I must provide the things that I desire accordingly. I must now sow a fruitful harvest. With all the material wishes that this life has at its disposal within my grasp, I must think of those things that would now make me smile. What? What else other than a throne with a tamed lion at my side. Servants and citizens adorning the foot of my throne with gifts and offerings. All of the citizens in stiff competition to see who could come up with the greatest gifts. As the recipient of these gifts, I can only wait and watch the results of this competition. Lavish ornaments of gold. The best harvested fruits. Clothes. Armor. Pictures. Statues of me, of course—the king. What would be the greatest gift for this king? A fitting queen.

Queen. One who encompasses all the qualities that are characteristic of a great woman. Beauty. Femininity. Submissiveness. Sensitivity. Tenderness. The smell of soap and perfume. The long hair corralled by a crown fit for this queen. Real gold laced uniform made of soft silk. As we listen to Aaron Hall's "I Want Your Body," the gold cups hold her breasts up, with this dress allowing her skin tone to show as her brown eyes stare into mine. Lips looking like the red or maybe a silicone pink, real close to red. You can see a string of her hair out of the side of the crown. Nails freshly manicured, beneath just as clean. Hands as soft as her bronze skin. I kiss her hand while pulling her close, and I can't resist her beauty and these qualities bestowed on this most beautiful queen. I look up at God and blow him a kiss because I'm very thankful for this reward.

I promise to be as sensitive and as affectionate as a king can be, and as protective as a king can be. While grabbing her hand, I ask her to have a seat next to my throne. She sits and crosses her legs as a queen would. Her smile is that of my dream. I take my seat. Proud, I am. She is mine. She loves me just the same. I am the only one who can make her feel this glow of love, and the feeling is mutual. No need to search any further. Nothing like her. I can relax; my heart is at ease. I don't have to worry about this queen. I don't have to come home to the sight of Madam in my bed. I don't have to worry about Steve or Adam either. I know what it took to get her. They would have to go through the same things, so when they finally start digging each other, I would probably have picked up on it. I would then try a "part B." If that didn't work, I would have no other choice but to return to being a soldier. My queen is gone; she has found a new king. Fortunately, once a king, always a king—to some queen.

Hierarchy of My Life

My life definitely has a hierarchy. The root to this hierarchy is God. Next is myself. Next is education. Next is work. Next is family. Happiness falls somewhere in between during different intervals every once in a while. Sometimes in this life but not all the time. I live by this hierarchy. This is my means to become successful, my way to stabilize my life, my way to ensure that everything will be OK. If things go bad, then I can resort to the first stage or the foundation of my hierarchy.

Today, there has been another mass shooting. I guess any smart person must think about the reasons for all the shootings as of late. Any God-loving human being would definitely inquire about these shootings. What is going on? Why? I guess if you aren't thinking about God, obviously you have to be thinking about something else: the devil. You also have to look at the devil's hierarchy. Devil, you, your house, your car, your job, your wife, your pride, your click. Things of this nature. Those who engage in mischief are usually the ones who are successful. Those who worship the devil are usually prosperous materially; so why not ride with the devil? I explained earlier that corruption and hypocrisy were the root to the demise of our culture.

The leniency that was intended to help has now begun to hurt our country. There must be an effort to correct all the ills that plague society. If the devil is going to be in charge, then get ready for destruction. If he has captured the minds of the masses, then America prepare for more of what has been going on lately. Believers in the prophecy of doom will attempt to fulfill this prophecy. The world is going to end. Yes, the signs are there. Seemingly, there are ways to prevent this occurrence. We must begin the process of ridding skeptics of doomsday thinking. God would never destroy the world totally. There will be revolts and things that we won't understand, but still there will be the opportunity to make things right.

There will always be the opportunity to repent. There will always be the opportunity to make amends for past sins. You see, the devil is all-powerful in creating havoc. He can also implement bad dreams in one's mind. How else could the devil reach angels other than by pretending to be an angel? Where does the devil come into play when we're talking about the doomsday theory? Does he have a role? Yes! This is where one has to be smart and see how the devil fits into this equation, and this attempt to totally confuse and destroy this world. Understand that being in accord with God requires constant praying. Every second and every minute, he must be in your equation for success. He must be at the root of your hierarchy. Believe this: by having God as the foundation for your hierarchy, he can ward off the devil. Because the devil can be a deed, a vision, a person, an action, and so forth, God allows you to detect the devil. This is all a big dream. Wake up!

Without controversy, God must be at the root of your hierarchy. This is point one, the most important point: God. Who is God? God is all that encompasses this world, right and wrong. You have to look at this life like mathematics, plusses and minuses. Like the criminal system, there are consequences for your actions. This is why it's important to be consistent and stay on the side with God. Stay good, and good things will happen to you. Get on the wrong side, and you know the deal. You see, the devil uses materials. God uses you. He expects for you to be able to withstand temptation. There's a greater reward for being faithful to God.

You may not see those rewards in this lifetime. Those rewards may not come in the form of materials. What is that reward? Everlasting life, heaven on the next planet. Wherever that may be. Whoever you may be. I'm sure it will be predetermined. It's just like if all the good students came from Harvard, then all the Harvard students would get the best jobs. There are trillions of lives out there waiting for some good saints. We have yet to figure out this wonderland because we have too many problems.

Me, I'm this little seed waiting to bloom, not sure if I will. It depends on the nurturing of another, the one who planted this seed. It depends on how much water I get, the food, the sunlight that I receive, and lots of things. It depends on this world and where I'm planted. My growth can be estimated by past tendencies, by seeds before me. Here I come. I'm growing. There is a drought; my growth becomes stagnant. Still I bloom. I'm a flower now. What do I do? Bloom, as any flower would. Bloom for the duration of this flower's life. I have all the physical qualities to bloom as beautiful as my physical efforts will allow.

My job. My job is to ensure that I am properly nourished. It is my job to make sure that I secure a means to take care of me and my family in the distant future. I have to have long-term plans. These long-term plans will be executed as a result of the success of my short-term plans. How well I plan will determine my standard of living once I, as a flower, become less beautiful when I bloom. When I start to shed leaves, begin to bend, and can't straighten up; when I'm unable to nourish myself, I must now depend on the resources that I have saved. As a flower of my type, I've done a good job, so the future doesn't worry me. I haven't wasted any time previously, so I'm OK with the prospect of growing old. My family. My mom. My dad. My kids. My wife. My sisters and brothers. My aunt and uncles. My nieces and nephews. My friends. My employees. My business partners. In this order, these are the people who need me. These are the people whom I will need. Not necessarily of the same seed, yet people I can trust and love. People whom I will gladly return to a seed for, people whom I enjoy being around. People who I know will give me all that I give them. Huh? Wait a minute—they come next.

My dreams. These are my aspirations that all of the above can assist me with. My dreams are facilitated by all of the above. My dream of being one of the most beautiful flowers keeps me pushing, keeps me planning, watering my roots. I have hope that during finer times and quiet times, the associations with my name will be those of high regard. This is my dream. I live the script that I think will be my legacy. My dream. My life. My God-given ability to make this flowery world a big bloom. Make us all alike. Even though we are all different, we are still all alike. We are all still flowers that will have different experiences. Some flowers might enjoy the company of other, different flowers. This is OK. Beauty is in the eye of the beholder. I simply have to make my dream come true. It is to be hoped that it will be enough for me.

Happiness. Happiness is the ultimate goal of every flower. It falls in between the levels in this hierarchy. It occurs occasionally along the way, every now and then. Happiness is the one thing that we all crave and desire. This is a reward issued out by God as a result of your faithfulness. Something so hard to come by, however something that comes so simple. Happiness can be having a spouse who loves you. A mate who cares about you. Both of you are in love and grow together, as husband and wife. You share all the hard times and the good times. Happiness can even be the purchase of a material fantasy. Happiness can be a union with God. Happiness can be the thought of things to come. It can be a combination of all the above. You should do whatever makes you happy. When you figure out everything, you will find that this was the original intent in the beginning: To be happy. To be stable and not have any of those things you worked for taken away. Being stable enables you to take pride in the fact that you worked hard to build this foundation. Stability also allows you to take pride in the fact that you're now in the process of going back to a seed and growing again and again. Everlasting happiness.

Maximum Output

I relax as would any tired individual. I lay down then see a light. I'm so tired, so pressed for energy, so this light amazes me. Having been through so much as of late leaves me cautiously optimistic of my journey and questioning my self-worth. Tired, I still must get up and push forward. I run toward the light, then stumble and fall. I get up and keep going, running. Not sure of where I'm going, in curious pursuit of this light at the end of the tunnel. Sweat now embraces my face. A tear falls into the wind, into the shadows of darkness. I keep running. I fall. I get up. I keep running, not as fast now; I'm growing weary of this journey that now seems to be leading to nowhere. I press on.

Other tears rush to join the other tear in the darkness. I keep running, and the light is now brighter. I guess I'm getting close to the end of this tunnel. I guess I'm almost there. I push harder and run faster. Already running my fastest, I push a little harder, hoping that I can move just a little faster, unaware of my bad knee, totally consumed by the brightness of this light. I can now see my shirt and my pants. I can see my hands swiftly pass through the dim light. I can see the darkness and the ice on the side of the cave.

My efforts are paying off. I push forward, not sure what lies ahead. What lies ahead? What is on the other side of this light? What if a cliff lies on the other side of this light? What if I just fall straight down? I keep running. I fall one more time and get up. I push one more time. I run. The light is getting brighter. I can see the end. I dive, not knowing where I might be going. Not knowing if there is some tribe or natives outside this cave that may kill me. Who cares? I've come too far to turn back. What is at the end? Damn! Same thing that was at the other end. I accept this bruise on my forehead, wipe off the dirt, then feel for my teeth. I get up, then look for a place that's hiring.

Right or Wrong, Never Right!

I knew this was going to be hard, but now it's even harder. Trying to keep my dignity and sanity. I try so hard to be me. Me, being this diverse dude who tries to reach out to others. Me, being this politician who has to promote diversity no one understands. No one understands me. I'm Black. I'm American. Is it possible to be both? I'm not sure. How can I be this American? How can I be me? I even feel like I'm not being me. I want to retreat back to the Black thing. Thankfully, there's strength in being me. I simply have to get the things I deserve and not keep getting those things taken away. I have to financially support myself, something so very hard in this life. Something that will take a long time. What a fight. What a life.

Is my diversity, diversity? Is my diversity selling out? Is my diversity right? Am I wrong for wanting diversity? No, I'm right and will continue to fight for diversity for the remainder of my life. You be the judge as to the righteousness or wrongfulness of my decision. Now, as my life starts to take shape, I can only smile. Smiling, knowing that my mission is not in vain. I know what I have done is right. I know that it's best for my country. Adversely, this won't be taken kindly by everyone. I just don't believe my intentions and thoughts will be taken in the right way, still unsure of the ending. David White called the other day, and it made me smile. I don't think I've ever been happier. He told me not to worry and that everything was going to be all right. It was good to know my efforts were beginning to pay off. I guess this was a reason to relax a little bit. I told you nobody was going to know how to take this story, no one was going to want to accept the fact that I'm just a good writer. I'm smarter than they are; that's a fact. I'm more creative than they are, more ambitious than they are. Here we go—I told you. People are positioning themselves for something I've worked hard to acquire. I guess when you look at all that has been taken away from you, it's kind of hard to believe that once again those things are going to be taken away. At the least they're going to try. I'm ready to deal with whatever. I've earned this and will fight to the end to keep it!

Once again, years of positioning, years of struggle. Now everyone is trying to see how they fit in. I guess this is what makes you not want to have kids. I kind of regret it now, but it's OK. I love my kids and know they love me. I know what it will take to perfect our system of government. I don't ask for anything I don't deserve; I just go out and get mine, humbly bearing the burden for others' misfortunes. Once again I'm very proud to be myself. Still very proud to be an American. I told them what it took. Now it's OK. This is my life.

My life to win or my life to lose. A life that I have went on by myself. I earned this. I waited on my friends and admirers to make a move, and nothing happened. I proceed by myself. That's why I exposed all the things that I did, so they could see clearly, hopefully, taking in why this life is so hard, or why this life is so easy. I don't believe this life has to be that hard for me. I'm skilled. Highly skilled. Highly educated. I earned this right to be rich. You feel me.

Wrongfulness would be giving everything that I earned to a bunch of people who didn't give a damn about me. What have you done for me? Yeah. What have you loaned me? I bet you can count the money I loaned you. I sit here wondering, *Whom can I call? Whom can I depend on?* No one. I'm alone in this battle. I wouldn't want them to loan me nothing. This is my life to win. Don't try to take something you haven't earned. It's all about money. I told you the problems and how we could solve them. You can even vote for me to solve them. I'm a politician, a writer, an entrepreneur positioned to be successful. I'm here to be what I told you I could be: a billionaire. Not giving away millions. Using my money for my well-being. We are all individuals with individual thinking. I accept that. One can't please everybody. I can please myself. You see, it's not about their rights or wrongs.

It's about you taking control of your life and making the decisions to do what is best for yourself.

Do what is best for Skip Flanagan. Have my business in order. Do what is best for me. If I want a house, then so be it. If I want a car, then so be it. I don't roll on public opinion; I used to. My life is a different kind of life. The rights and wrongs in my life don't revolve around someone else's perception of what right and wrong is. I know what to do. I have a plan, and this is that plan. Being positioned for millions through writing, through music. Hey, here I come again. I could never be right to everybody because if you ask me, they are all wrong. I would never let my mother suffer. I would never not take my family into account as far as success goes. My success will benefit my loved ones, my friends, and causes that are important to me. The righteousness of my decisions will not be able to be measured right now; it'll take a while. The wrongfulness has already been established. You're wrong before you're right. Standing alone, I can handle the results of my decisions, individually to me. No one comes close to being the man that I am. I am Skip Flanagan. I am Grassroots Empire. I am. Right or wrong?

Conspiracy or Bad Legislation?

As I sit back and anticipate the hard-earned results of my efforts, I can only wonder about the readers that are reading my works, if any. I'm nervous. I'm scared. I'm Black. I'm young. I don't know what is going on. I'm curious. I did what I felt was right. I said things that my heart directed me to, knowing I've done God's will. Still, I'm unsure that I'll receive the reward that any God-loving man would desire: the love of those you have reached out to help. In this case, misinformed African Americans and peace-seeking Americans.

As a result of wretched seeping of the mind, constant study, sleepless nights, and dangerous situations, I'm now knowledgeable of the ills that plague America. In no way am I stupid to the fact that others may see these same problems. My neighbors, my teachers, my congresspeople, my mayor, my president, and I have to be aware of these problems. I believe that these problems can be solved by changes in legislation and by a change in thinking. Seriously, I must ask myself, Is the well-being of all Americans at the heart of the lawmakers of America? Do the laws benefit the poor? Is it the goal of this country to make everyone equal? I don't know.

Is there a conspiracy against people of color? Does the fault lie in the inability of minority politicians to successfully get across their points? Is it bad legislation? I don't know. I believe that the judges and lawmakers have to be more creative in their attempts to enact laws. I think there must be some detailed research into the long-term effects of the decision to enact certain laws. We live in a society that is based on capital. We live in a society that is based on work. The laws are enacted, implemented, and further executed under the assumption that every person is a productive individual in society. Penalties are imposed, for instance.

Everything that is done is done under the assumption that the person committing the violation has some form of money.

To exist costs. Property is preowned, and to lease or rent property requires a fee. Having kids costs. A doctor bill is immediately imposed on the parents of the kid. Child support immediately follows. The assumption is that this couple will earn at least fifty dollars per week to take care of this kid, not counting rent money, car note, and utilities. I believe that it's totally impossible to take care of two homes unless you're rich. If careers are not important, and the majority of minorities have not and will not be attending college, then entry-level jobs and pay are what they will be getting. So how in the world are they going to pay for rent, utilities, child support, insurance, car registration, food, gas, and any other expense? This is where the knowledge of the situation is necessary.

I mean the knowledge that we live in a democracy founded on jobs, existing jobs, and jobs created. The success of this democracy is also based on the success of the economy, the abundance of capital in circulation. It's based on spending, which allows for businesses and individuals to prosper. In compliance, all of the above must be based on legal circulation and generate capital. Unlawful activities interfere with the competition and continual economic growth, smothering out potential businesses. Many are now gone, as well as prospective employees. Thus, we want to look at this situation from a legal perspective. Even though the problems are rooted in illegal activities, there must be a vision of success. There must be examples of success. There must be the equal opportunity for all citizens of this great country. People have been hollering conspiracy for years. Are their cries warranted? I don't know. I guess you have to look at each cry individually. For there to be a conspiracy, we have to first look at what has taken place in the past so we can determine the cause of the present conditions.

Unemployment. The lack of employment will often supports the conspiracy cry. The jobs. The type of jobs and the amount of money being paid to the individuals with the same qualifications. There must first be a desire to work. A desire to become a productive citizen. A desire to do right. A desire to be someone special. A desire to be American. An attempt to survive, whereas work is the only way to generate capital in a capitalistic society. First, one must have faith in the democracy. One has to believe that in this democracy, opportunities are equally accessible to each and every American citizen.

These opportunities must be present without bias or favor. I recall in my earlier days when everyone used to work. When my friends and I went to look for jobs, we would wear our best clothes. Nowadays, job hunters wear anything. They go to job interviews in shorts or whatever they want to wear. I had a certain amount of respect for the employer. Now, guys assume that they either have to work, or it's the duty of the employer to find them and employ them. That's not the way it works. Jobs and businesses are not guaranteed. Profit is not guaranteed.

Opportunity isn't guaranteed, and if you get the job, you have to respect the employer and act like you are appreciative that the company hired you. You further have to take pride in the fact that you want to do your job well, or you will be fired. There are many things to learn in society. Educating yourself is the best thing that a person can do. This is the only way that we will understand the importance of working and the order of this society. There's no other way that one can appreciate work and further see the opportunities that exist.

Minds will forever be clouded concerning the means of acquiring and understanding how to live in America and be happy. This will forever be vague to many, as a result of the nonexistence of education and knowledge. Planning and investing will forever seem to be tumultuous mountains to those who fall into this category; these things go along with long-term goals and preparation for quality living. The only things to look forward to for the uneducated are jail and mischief. No work. No eating. Lots of killing and jail time. Now they're having a debate about the death penalty.

There are some vicious killers out there. Robbers. Criminals. It really puts you in a bad situation. I was watching *Dateline*, and a Black guy was given the death penalty for killing a cop. I thought about the life that was taken. The cop's life. The cop's family. As a Black American, I can see into the minds of Black Americans. I could see directly into this guy's heart. I knew he was a killer. I've seen guys go to prison and come out, knowing full well what the guy is going through.

Jail is definitely a better life than the life that this individual was probably living. There is now more pressure to be someone. There is now more pressure to catch up and be a citizen. There is no chance of getting away with another murder. In his case, murder was something he can take pride in. Murder is trivial because the more murders he commits, the more self-esteem he will have. To him, bad is good. Good is bad. Murder to a God-loving individual is the worst sin a person can commit. I would dread having to kill someone over some type of material. I don't think I could. However, who knows what I would do when enraged? Anyone is capable. A seven-year-old is capable. The truth is we're in a subtle war against each other. The climate is already established. The police are the enemy. This is the thinking.

The government is the cause of all the evils that plague America. The chance of succeeding is very small. I'm Black. The statistics show that the chances of me succeeding are slim to none. The chances of being incarcerated are also very high. So is there a conspiracy?

Can Black Americans succeed? Yes. There are thousands— no, millions of Black Americans who are doing well. Millions of compatriots who have never had a dangerous encounter with a violent felon. So who are these guys who are incarcerated? Who are these new felons? It's my thinking that this new influx of criminals are would-be athletes, doctors, and lawyers. Individuals who were cast out, who probably just needed a little guidance, just one more chance. This goes back to my thinking that inner-city ghettos' acceptance of this new lifestyle isn't helping and is only hurting.

Counterproductive: the thought that gangsterism is the standard for Black America. The thought that the tougher you are, the better you are. I don't think that it's a secret what most Black Americans think. They say the things on tapes. I think if drugs were legalized, the sale of drugs would go down. These abject thinkers would feel like what they were doing is right and therefore rebel against it. You see, they want to do what they're not supposed to do. Mom says, "Hey, pull your pants up!" The kid looks. As soon as he gets outside, he pulls his pants down. He will accidentally come home with his pants down. Eventually, conditioning Mom to accept his trifling act. Other bad habits are soon to follow this act, or this part of Black culture.

Given an overall look at the habits and tendencies in the Black community, I can see the direction that Black Americans have turned. I can see how the effects of psychological and physical ills have affected the progress of Black Americans. Success is easy if there are no obstacles. African Americans have to overcome lots of hurdles, and usually these hurdles are self-imposed. There is an overall rebellion against education. Anything that can help is associated with White Americans, so Black Americans therefore rebel against it. Education, working, speaking properly—all things that are a part of the hierarchy for success. All things that a relatively unintelligent youth has now taken for granted and has therefore rebelled against.

The hierarchy of life, which must be adhered to in order for anyone to be successful. Young White Americans' fascination with this lifestyle also creates a decline in the moral standard of America. Young White Americans simply wanting to be friends. Young White Americans simply attempting to encourage dialogue with their Black American friends. As I continue to research the ills that plague Black inner cities, I'm unable to leave out the fact that the thirst to be rich is the root of all the evil. The want for money. The desire to be rich. The lack of the knowledge of what it takes to be rich. The impatience that consistently exists in these neighborhoods. What if they just wanted to survive? Well, a good job is not easy to find. Especially if you have dropped out of school and have no form of education.

Education—remember that word. When I was growing up,

there was a way that everyone was distinguished. You were popular because you were an athlete. If you weren't an athlete, then you were known because you could dance well. You sometimes knew others because they drove their moms' cars. Yes, and you did know who the thugs were. Everybody wasn't a thug. When we were in the classroom, we saw the thugs standing outside by the fence. They usually ganged up and beat up someone for some reason or another. They were thugs. You knew who they were. Everybody wasn't a thug. Life was fun. The girls were nice, and they made sure they kept themselves in order. They had class; there was no way that you were going to have sex with one of the girls who went to class every day.

Oral sex was totally out of the question. All girls were not freaks. You knew who the freaks were; they routinely strolled down the sidewalk. At noon, you could look out the window and see them. You definitely didn't call a girl a bitch—no way. Cursing was not even prevalent. You seldom used cuss words because it wasn't classy. Everybody didn't curse. We went to the games. We looked forward to going to school, playing the crosstown rivals, and seeing old alumni at the games. We even sought our old teachers in hopes of sharing our success with them, as well as classmates. School was a major part of the hierarchy of life, a detailed hierarchy that was a straight line to success. Life was fun. Now, kids aren't even making it to school. They stay home and create havoc on the corner down the street from the house. What kind of stuff is that? I guess all these problems originate at the home front.

When I was growing up, the neighbor could whoop us. The neighbors would definitely call the house if they saw that we weren't at school. What has happened in the hood? Let's look at the legislation. It is no longer OK to discipline your children. Paddling or any form of physical disciplining is considered abuse. I believe in disciplining, and paddling as a form of disciplining. I remember when my junior high school coach used to paddle us. He had one of those paddles with the holes in it. He used to tear us up! I didn't like being paddled, so I didn't do anything wrong.

I was full of fear, yet I operated with this fear of messing up, so I didn't mess up. I believe that kids need to have some form of fear in them.

Today's kids don't have any fear. The intent of the legislation that prohibits physical disciplining may have been sincere in its attempt to protect the kid. Yet as with many other forms of legislation, such as welfare, the original intent has been mistaken. Consequently, this good has now turned into a bad. Furthermore, with kids having no fear of their parents, what would be an incentive to do right? I don't think Black American kids are prepared for the option of not getting an education. They usually have no inheritances or anything of the sort, so a life as a criminal is an easy out. Especially if this lifestyle is being glorified. Especially if this bad can generate a form of capital or a means of taking care of him.

This life as a thug is good, it's accepted by the majority. It's not prohibited, so it's OK. In addition, it's an easy way out. The easiest thing in the world to do is quit. That's all you have to do: lie down and don't get up. It's cool to be a failure. You even have someone to blame: the government. They took paddling out of schools. They took prayer out of schools. They implemented legislation with the intent to help. This legislation is now being used to incriminate the government. Do you feel me? Look at the original intent of the legislation. Then look at the individual. Look at the individuals.

I believe that there are ills that plague the Black neighborhoods. Yet these poignant nuisances are created by these same individuals. Yes, there are conspiracy theories that point to the government putting drugs in the neighborhood. Well, why do you still fool with it? Whom do you blame? There are other conspiracy theories that others have brought up. So what? Those facts have been established. Let's move on. It is my belief that there are solutions to these problems. The solution to most of these problems can be solved at the polls. One solution is to have more Black Americans attempting to become politicians, policeman, governors, and jobs of this nature. It is also the duty of citizens to make sure that the officials that they elects have the issues of the community at heart. They must have those issues on their agenda and in their hearts. If not, then your civic club and organizations should be formed by you, the businessman, the citizen, to deter the ills of your community.

A difficult task. Moreover, a chance to counter the so-called conspiracy and maybe even make history—positive history. Voting is also a part of this hierarchy. You're a citizen, and you have to participate. You have to be a part of this change. First, you have to have knowledge of the ills, the legal and logical solutions with the possibility of successful implementation. This is America, and you're free. Free to assist in change. Free to run for president if that is your choice. It's not going to be easy. Neither was the abolition of slavery. Neither was the abolition of polio. Neither was the winning of Vietnam. Neither was the writing of the constitution. Shut up. You already quit. There is no conspiracy that cannot be countered, addressed, and eliminated by proper legislation or mass movements. What are you going to do? What do you believe? This is where we're at. Where are we going?

Politicians Aren't Listening

I seem to think that politicians are not getting the message when it comes to diversity and change. During a time when the majority of homelanders are desperately seeking change, the present politicians are insensitive to their cries. This irresponsibility and insensitivity should be remembered and reflective in the poll results in the next election. Americans as a whole are great individuals. When you look at how many countryman rallied around Bill Clinton and his concept of change, one was rewarded with an insight to the hearts of America. Collectively, Bill Clinton's presidency and the years in which he was president were some interesting times that were marred by conspiracies and misdeeds. Still, it's the beginning of things to come.

I believe that the majority of Americans are still ready to add to this new era of reconciliation and goodwill, of God's will. I haven't met anyone who wants to go to hell. Contemptuously, politicians continue to disregard the views and interests of the American people. That trend will definitely come back to haunt them.

Land of the Free, Home of the Brave—America

The words "Land of the free, home of the brave" ring with the sound of inclusion as far as one can see. I believe that similar to politicians, most have come to America and bought into the concept of supremacy. I think we all need to reconsider what being American is. I don't know how many times I will have to say that we need to have a one million American march so that we can detail the American culture. A detailed culture that is very complex, yet a standard that is just and detailed. Let me once again say, I love America, and I love Americans. Still, there are so many problems that are prevalent and need to be eradicated from our society.

Blaming failure on White Americans is a major cop-out that should be eradicated. The sky is the limit in the land of the free and the home of the Brave. Brilliance, technology, and expertise are also things that assist in the establishment of success and failure. Accept the terms and conditions of the United States. Why can't we accept the fact that White Americans are skilled at something? We are quietly attempting to squeeze the White Americans out of society. Have we noticed? Do White Americans have to play down their expertise in order to be accepted by their own, and by people around the world? I don't think so. I, a Black American, have the utmost respect for White Americans. They get no credit for all that they bring to the table for the world. I guess when you implement the bad legislation as well as the good legislation, blame can only lie with the majority. It's time to quit the supremacy on all sides of the table and focus on being one, as I stated in my first book.

Consistency is very important. Consistency in what you believe and your ability to get your point across is essential to your being who you say you are. I stand alone on this battle.

No warriors with me. Way out on a limb. My integrity to be doubted. My name to be ruined. Scorched by small minds that don't understand or see what I see. The power of education and how knowledge holds the key to understanding in a country that is based on this hierarchy of success. All Americans must buy into this hierarchy, and God, knowledge, and wisdom are the root of this hierarchy. Understanding and being able to see the good in the very people who have enabled us to have a country that is void of slavery and civil unrest. Never to see civil unrest and the possibility of a bomb touching ground in the United States.

A country where you, as a result of being a citizen, can now use the earth and its resources to make a living. Pursuing the finer things in life, being able to make those things a reality. Do you believe? You can even get a house through the government: Section 8. Free, if you have children who aren't being taken care of. If you're hungry, you can get food stamps for food. No one should ever be hungry in America. There are places that will even pay your utilities. Homes and cars are the prize winnings in this quest for the American dream now accessible to you. If this is what you want, what's the problem? This will be given to you to comfort your failure. As a headstrong individual, I've always been able to get anything in this life. I can only watch and observe how Section 8 thinking has inhibited mainstream America, consuming as well as aiding those with the intent of stealing what they couldn't get honestly.

I'm OK with the system, realizing that there are things that need to be changed. Judge Koch said, "You can overcome it!" I believe it and have shown it. I am one of the more intellectually sound yet physically talented individuals in society. I'm not the prettiest, but I'm one of the hardest working, constantly striving to be perfect. If the standard has been established by one of my White American brothers, friends, or peers, then so shall I be like him. I'm smart enough to know better than to fall into this desolate trap of hopelessness. I'm smart enough to see a better America, a progressive America. I am free in body, soul, and in heart. I fully understand the intent of the laws of this land, so I adhere and conform.

My conforming doesn't mean this is the beginning of my failure. Instead, I have now taken the initiative to begin the process of following the hierarchy to success. I have to be humble to keep from killing those more violent. I have to practice diplomacy and be smart enough to avoid the immoral, exhibiting patience and serving God. God's will is to tell the truth. I have the same strength in telling the truth for Black Americans, as I'll have in telling the truth about White Americans. We are family. The truth is the most powerful tool in existence in this free world. The evils of hatred are the most dangerous and most threatening forces in this world. Those evils are like a steel door on a dope house, not allowing entrance for anyone other than those of their likeness. I can't get in.

I'm stuck in this America. I'm stranded and corralled like a studhorse in the field. Ride me to the top. I stand alone, physically and mentally capable of taking on any foe, smart enough to know the truth, willing to die for these truths. Death by another American? No, another unruly citizen in this great America. "Land of the free, home of the brave." Brave I am!

Voilà!

Failure. The act of falling and not getting up. The act of conceding defeat and the acceptance of the consequences that accompany this act. The realities of life and the turmoil that exists in this country are now upon the masses. I'm now ordained by the almighty God to be able to verbally convey this accumulation of knowledge and wisdom to many other misinformed, misguided Americans. During a time where it's OK to join an extremist group. During a time when people are more inclined to be receptive to the evils of this world. Many are ready to concede death by any means necessary.

This failure is now being justified by their belief in theory that the world is going to end in the year 2000. Given one's belief in the Bible and one's dependence on the Bible as a book by which all walks of life must live by, the loyalty in their beliefs creates this atmosphere of hopelessness. A sense of urgency and impatience follows as one attaches to this misery—biblical justification for systematic killings and systematic genocide. Who is evil? Who is the devil? This depends on the individual and on the interpretation of the scripture. The year 2000 is upon us. Now what?

There is now a cry to release all nonviolent prisoners. I've learned a lot. As with everything else, cocaine use is really not important. It is a choice in America—a bad choice. I feel as though some of the sentences are too harsh for drug crimes. However, in my case, I feel I'm an example of how this system has worked. Once again we must go back to the original intent of the legislation. That intent is to deter crime and get rid of drugs, something that is almost impossible. Someone is going to find a way to get those drugs.

My observation of the drug war and its effects have shown once an addict, always an addict. The addicts use cocaine as an excuse to not continue with life, using cocaine addiction as an excuse for failure. Let's take a look at other countries. In one country, I'm not sure which country it was, but the country puts people in a special home if they're considered not fit for society. These are citizens who are considered "not perfect." Those with basic speech defects and minor handicaps. These so-called undesirables are put in a special center for the nonproductive. If such was the case in America, many would not be fit for society. I guess this new influx of prisoners are those outcasts. Do you feel me? There is a choice here: to or not to. So now you have all the consumers and entrepreneurs in jail. All are drug free with ample time to think about their wrongdoings. All have ample time to think about what to do next.

Some are already conditioned to do only what they know, and they will immediately go back to doing what they were doing when they went to jail. Let's take a look at a thirty-eight-year-old drug addict. He has been in jail for six years. He gets out and tries to work. The workplace has changed. He can't get a good job because of his criminal record. He can't get an apartment because of his criminal record. He cannot vote because of his criminal record. He has to stay with a friend. He has to operate with a sense of urgency now because he has to pay rent to his friend. Today's women want what they can see now. They want to be taken care of, so how can this ex-con survive? The thought of not being able to get those things necessary to make him happy kicks patience out the window. No more patience. What now?

Self-esteem is important. Everyone wants to be important to someone. People hope that their friends have a favorable opinion of them. Everyone wanting to be special, wanting to have some form of power. Most people will do anything to get power. Power is that which is feared. Thus, power is respected. Power comes from many different sources: money, intelligence, beauty, being member of an organization or extremist group. What choice do you think a convicted felon would choose? How can someone who has spent the majority of his time to get slicker cheat or beat the system? This thinking, this need to be someone but not knowing how to become it. A willingness to accept any lifestyle or membership that the general public can associate with becomes the result. What else could deter this new mission to be a normal citizen in a society where the standards of success are measured by the number of materials you have? When in a society, beauty is a part of this standard. What can make one change one's way of life, especially when the majority of the minority has accepted their lifestyle as acceptable?

Unfortunately, the reality of it all is that no one cares. No one gives a damn unless one has the world. How will you be measured in a world where you are only as good as your street reputation, your jail reputation, or those great things people will say at your funeral? One can only attempt to add to one's legacy. A life of uncertainty. A life that no one seems to care about. A phenomenon. A drastic change in your life that is the result of a political movement, or natural change, for the better in your life. Man, I guess this is hard right here. If AIDS is not cured within the next six years, we will be seeing a new natural holocaust. I guess this world is about to end. Get ready for a phenomenon or a holocaust. This is one more knife in the bucket.

I guess everyone is tired of all these bad endings. I guess this is why peace and racism are towers of turmoil; clouding the peace process indefinitely. You see, someone is going to blame someone. Who is going to take the blame for this one? A tough dilemma for all Americans and people around the world. This is a world problem that deserves urgent attention. There is a sense of urgency that should be attached to this problem. Don't you think so?

Combine this with the other problems. Cancer. Drugs. Unemployment. Lack of an education. Lack of cultural values. Lack of knowledge. Then voilà! You feel me? Don't give up. Romance for now is put on hold. Too much to lose. Patience once again kicked in the butt. The unknown has a tight grasp on you. Love a dream. Life is hell, as we wait on a miracle. Not necessarily a miracle, just a small phenomenon, or a servant to come along and get rid of the roadblock in the middle of the street. Let's not blame anyone or even consider the theories. Let us find a solution to all the problems that interfere in the establishment of peace. Let us live for as long as God wants us to. We need a phenomenon. Voilà! God is that phenomenon. Smile.

Peace—A Process

Peace: a state of quietness. A state of happiness. A state of love and joy. A state of normalcy and contentment with your present self and your existing situation. This peace leads to goodwill toward others. This creates situations of nonviolence. It deters crime, encourages dialogue among people who are presented with life-threatening situations, and creates quiet. Peace is the existence of no problems. Some other world. Space, maybe, but even space has explosions. The president wants peace. People in Israel sign peace accords. Does everyone want peace? No way, buddy. Some people worship the devil.

This devil worshipping is really easy to get entangled in if you don't believe in God. The forces of good and evil are usually easily distinguishable but not always. The process of getting into heaven is a slow one. One that requires grooming. One that requires teaching and understanding as one is prepared to endure the forces of evil. One's impatience and sense of urgency present the opportunity for one to join the army of evil. The devil and God use similar tools in their attempts to win followers. The means for acceptance is rather difficult for both sides. Murder is on one side. Sacrifice, suffering, and patience are on the other side. One is accepted on either side. Consistency in your work is a must.

What is the goal of peace? We have to first look at the reasons why there is no peace. One, money. Two, freedom. Three, religion. All are obstacles that interfere with the peace process. Money can pay for all the things necessary for one to survive—homes, cars, food, and almost anything on this planet. Love. Freedom is the ability to pursue all your dreams. Freedom is the ability to go and come as one pleases. Freedom is the ability to speak one's mind. Freedom is having the option of becoming rich. Freedom is also the ability to choose not to become rich. Freedom is the option of living a simple life. Freedom is the ability to fail and try again. Freedom is being able to jump in the pool and relax, or skip work. Freedom is the ability to dream and participate in the manifestation of that dream.

Religion is a part of the process and hierarchy of peace. Religion is one of the greatest causes of death in the world. *Religion.* What did you say? When one thinks of the world, one must think about the problems of this world. Some problems, or most problems, that take place in this world can be solved by some other means. We must allow the unknown to deal with the unknown—the unknown forces of evil, I might add. When one thinks about this life, one has to think in terms of right and wrong. Everyone wants to be as close to perfect as godly possible. Everyone longs to have access to all the things or material possessions that exist on this earth, especially the ones that are available in this country. Being religious is the act of repeating something over and over again.

Religious people believe that their means of establishing a relationship with God is the best means in known existence. I can respect that. Anything that gives one peace of mind and promise of eternal life should be respected, as long as one isn't a part of an extremist group. Hate cannot be in the process or the establishment of peace. One must humble oneself and accept the dialogue that goes along with the process of initiating peace. The ultimate goal is to have peace of mind and some form of self-worth. Ultimately, we all want world peace and total happiness. The initial goal is God's will in the beginning. I look at peace in a lot of different ways. Peace is sort of like the Grand Canyon. There are a whole lot of cliffs. Everyone has the freedom and the choice to jump off the cliff or remain still, to obey the laws of nature. One can imagine lots of near-death scenarios. One can easily kill oneself. Furthermore, the choice of being righteous and attempting to do things that facilitate peace is the choice of each individual person. Can we have peace? I don't know. Acquiring peace is a process.

There is a day-by-day attempt to get rid of all those who oppose peace, destroying those things that create civil unrest, and facilitating situations that don't allow peace. War is war. Peace is just a temporary state that substitutes in the absence of war. Peace is something that we all dream about, something that we all want. It is a distant reality at best. War is the worst-case scenario. We just have to keep working at peace. Day by day. Step by step. Treaty after treaty. Dream after dream. Such is this life.

If I Were a Kid

I wonder what I would do if I were a kid in this new world, in this new order, in this new country. A country with a multitude of new thinkers. A country and a world that I now must predict what will be new in years to come. I must anticipate the coming of this new millennium. I must prepare to deal with the present as well as the new technologies that will be presented to me, as well as the rest of society. I have to prepare to be competitive with other citizens in the workforce and on this earth. If I were a kid, I would cherish being showered with the basic necessities of life. A beautiful new bed. A cradle. Lots and lots of toys. Food of all kinds. Lots of milk. No problems. No job. No worries. Nobody to dislike me. Lots of hugs, lots of kisses. My new job is to listen and observe.

I must attempt only to see how I fit in this equation called life. I must shape only my conversation to this audience that I'll be observing over the next three years, my family. I hope that they have the adequate resources to be able to take care of me. Me, this kid. Me, the most precious thing to their knowledge. If I were a kid, I would encourage my parents to feed me a lot of milk and vegetables. Lots of cereal. I would encourage my dad to work hard and sometimes take me with him, so that I could observe his struggle.

I would ask Mom to not curse so much, and I'd ask Dad to be more diplomatic. I would ask the police to come a little quicker on weekends. I would ask my dad's employer to make sure to get Dad that Christmas bonus. I would ask my aunts and uncles to come by more and bring their families, seeing that we all need to get to know each other better. We have to have a family structure. I would constantly remind my mom the importance of speaking with proper grammar. I'm listening. I would preach to my mom the importance of playing more inspirational music, because this will assist in shaping my character. I would tell my family to listen to the older generation of songs and carefully pick and choose the rap songs that they played. I would tell them to get me a poster of Brandy and Halle Berry so that I could put them on my wall. I would encourage them to watch more of *Baywatch* and Pamela Anderson. I would tell them to turn the television to ABC at 9:00 p.m. Houston time and let it stay on until *Jimmy Kimmel Live!* went off. I would tell them to buy me a computer because I want to be a writer. I would ask that they not talk too much about the racism and the thugs in the neighborhood because this is useless knowledge. I don't need it; I'll learn about that later.

Instead, I would encourage them to make sure that I turn out perfect. Everybody doesn't have to make mistakes or go to jail to have a successful life. It's OK to be perfect. There will be other nearly perfect individuals. That is where I will belong. If I were a kid, I would encourage my mom to travel. Go to Mecca, Canada, Hawaii. Stay away from hostile territories. I would ask them to reach for the stars and not to take for granted the fact that we had to save enough money so we could one day ride the space shuttle. I would ask them to buy me some Skip Flanagan apparel because he is now my hero. He is a role model. I would ask my parents to move out of the ghetto to somewhere safe. I would ask my parents to be sure to send me to integrated schools so that I could learn more about others. I would ask my parents to start saving for me to go to college, because this is a part of the hierarchy to success. I would further ask my parents to not rush me into anything because I am a kid.

I would like to enjoy these fourteen years while they last. I would ask my parents to be careful in this dangerous world. I would tell my parents not to take this wisdom for granted because their son is a genius. Yes, I have been bestowed with a vast amount of knowledge and wisdom. Their son possesses high-octane intellect. The vastness of my thoughts and intellect are immeasurable by small minds. These minds are totally unable to compute the importance of the knowledge and wisdom that a God-ordained mind can convey to less intelligent individuals. I am the recipient of such a great gift, the greatest gift.

Subsequently, I'm smart enough to realize—you must remember I'm a genius—that this knowledge is useless if not put in print and used to benefit this world. If not, then I'm just another kid. Just like one of those child geniuses who was unable to nurture and shape the mind of knowledge that God bestowed equal amounts of knowledge in this other kid. God is simply waiting for the kid to summon up the gift and powers that he has given him. That kid chose not to. I can't worry about that kid. I must continue to water my roots. I must continue to nurture my thoughts. I would ask my parents to give me a vocabulary word each day so that I can have something to retrieve if I need to engage in more complex forms of communication or fellowship. I would tell my parents to work hard and prepare a way for me, because it won't be long before I'm an adult. I would tell them that whatever they didn't take care of, I will be back to finish. I would reiterate that we are family and must stick together. I would talk to them about the importance of our family and how we must do family-orientated things.

I must make them aware that I don't mind riding in the stroller for long periods of time. I would tell them that I forgot about the time they left me in the car; it was very hot. I would further remind them that this is against the law. If I were a kid, I would enjoy my life as a kid. I would play the new Dreamcast and Nintendo games. I would play hide and go seek. I would play kickball. I would play football—tackle on grass, and touch on cement. I would buy a real basketball goal and advise them to take down the bicycle rim. I would enjoy being this kid sustained by all the problems being solved in the lifetime before this one. I would prepare myself to deal with these new problems. I won't ruin my childhood by experimenting and not being cautious. I would casually observe and continue being a kid. I wouldn't fall short on awareness.

If I were a kid, I would ask my parents to take me to church. A church that was not an organization. A church that believed in God. A church that didn't believe in killing. A church that was progressive and receptive to change. A church that allowed members to speak sometimes. A church based on the truth. A church that used the Holy Bible, knowing that so many great individuals participated in the creation of this great book. Last, once I've graduated, I would thank my parents for their love and guidance through the years, knowing my life as a kid is now about to end. I would kiss them both, then pack my bags and be off to college.

College is a part of the hierarchy to success. I would ask them for one last favor: a conservative vehicle so that I could get around while I'm in college. I would further write a letter to Halle Berry, asking her If we could go out. I would cut out a picture of her and put it next to a picture of me. She would be my inspiration. She is my inspiration. I would now, as an adult, put my best foot forward. I'm smart enough to know that this is possible because I have been consistently at my best for many years. I'm smart enough to know that success does not occur by luck but instead by persistence.

I would now reevaluate where I stand. Then I'd take a look back at my childhood years and say, "Damn, that was fun!" I would shed one last tear, knowing those days will never come again. I would cherish these days as a kid, forever being grateful to my parents as I now move on. Thankful to be a citizen. Thankful that I, an American, can wear the colors of the flag proudly. Me, an American citizen. Now I'm able to pursue the American dream, with no reason to believe that this dream is not in my reach.

Yet that was as a kid. I'm now an adult. What now?

High-Octane Intellect

Constantly seeping and searching of the mind. Constantly searching for answers. Constantly trying to find solutions to your life's problems. Constantly trying to say something that can really win over that loved one. The brain as we see it in our science books, this small mass of pink lumps. These lumps full of pulses and this small light of blue and all colors. This light being life, something like a cosmo or something. This brain surrounded by water and a protective shell. Anything else is useless matter. Probably something put there as a result of missing the flow of fluids to the large intestine. Somewhere in there is the super X chromosome.

Somewhere in there is the reason that my mind thinks deeper than most, like only a few others. Those few others probably are scientists or nuclear physicists. I'm just an abnormal citizen. I'm just an American. As a result of struggle, I must constantly search the deepest crevices over and over and over again in my mind. If I miss, then I search again in my attempt to come up with solutions and answers to some of life's most complex dilemmas.

I'm a brother who's willing to put out the maximum amount of output that's necessary to come up with solutions and answers to my life. I simply think deep, deep into the higher levels of thought. The infinite space of storage allowed for by the human brain is a subcompartment of untapped knowledge waiting for a new generation. My liking is unto a well, tapped by myself, unwilling to wait on the searches of others. I am one with high-octane intellect. My disposition is kind of strange. I'm a yardman with visions of having a top-notch lawn service. Harshly, I'm sometimes forced to consider other options. Still, I'm one of the greatest writers of the century, forced only to be patient and put together a package for other's enjoyment. The accumulation of my knowledge and wisdom are prerequisites to be able to blurt out the type of responses that I reserved for the likes of Michelangelo, the great Albert Einstein, even the great Spike Lee. Fresh into a new era and a new generation that thinks a lot differently.

I have the added ability to speak with persuasion. Others are unable to see how to profit off this wisdom and can only observe and be patient. I'm wise enough to tear down any boundary, positioning myself to be the facilitator of my own dreams. Never in my wildest dreams did I think that change would be so difficult. Such is this world, the monetary beneficiary of hopelessness and poverty. Wealth comes in the form of poverty. The downside. The backside. This world. Is that this country? Is that this state? What a world. Does anyone know the solution? Does anyone care? So many times we will all miss, because we are unwilling to accept the source of the good news. Jesus brought the good news years ago. No Mercedes-Benz.

Dwelling among the poor unselfishly. No one knew the power of his mission until his death. Until this day. As a brother of him, I'm humbled by his sacrifice. I'm now positioned to do the same, and so are so many others, constantly asking the world, Why? Sometimes wanting to challenge the Supreme Being. Sensibly, one would be foolish to extend this great wrath of injustice. We live on, in a world that is totally dependent on the circulation of currency. Where does a God-loving servant fit? Down on my knees, praying. Hoping for an end to the hopelessness that has struck so many, the pain and agony of day-to-day life. These problems that are nothing to smile about. If you were the recipient of these injustices, you would know what I'm saying. Hell is definitely on Earth; just ask some people. Everything is not pretty.

Life is a struggle, and we simply have to endure. Endure the hardships, striving to solve the things that we have the power to solve. What about those of us who aren't pretty? Do we deserve anything other than suffering? Do we deserve anything other than poverty? I don't know. Always know that I love you and will fight alongside you, no matter who you are or where you are. We are family. This is for you. We are going to make it. When we make it, we're going to stop and pray, giving thanks to the One who know delivered us from all these problems. Though we are unaware of what we have done in times previous, we can only sift through this new rash of problems.

This new generation of bad luck. Contrite we are. Humble we are. Yet happy we cannot be. Happiness is a distant reality for someone like me. Freedom is now also a distant reality, as I often doubt my self-worth. This worth is zero, because the means of this establishment are far away from me, out of my reach. Meanwhile, the devil has a firm grip on those around me. Do I question the man? No. I simply pray that the end is near. I don't change but march forward, continuing as would any child of God. Still, I'm searching the dark sides of my inner brain for a logical solution to my own problems. Selfish now, because I'm entrapped by the force of poverty. I once again fall, not wanting to give up. Even though the realization is that staying down is the easiest thing to do.

I'm fearful of the consequences of my failure, but I'm up again and on my way. My hopes are slightly dimmed by the forces of evil that have a firm grip on my confidence that I will succeed. I'm up, like a boxer in the eleventh round! I can't quit! The door to hell is wide open, and there's a big party going on in there. Should I go in? Hell, no! I turn around and steer my vehicle in the right direction, pushing on is a must. There is a winner's circle. There is Halle. I smile, embracing the thought that a woman of this nature is truly a possibility, but only if I'm successful.

Me, being a king now, deserves this new queen. Logically, is this a prerequisite to happiness? I don't know. Even so, I know now that these are not important things. Now, as essentially the evaluator of others' intellect around me, stabilizing and esteeming my intellect is a must. I'm assertively corralling my intellect for the well-being of humanity, positioning my intellect for God's will, using this intellect for the benefit of my community. I observe the competition and fellow laborers, inquisitors who use their minds to become lawyers, philanthropists who use their knowledge to feed the homeless. I must press to nurture my intellect to help this world. There is basically nothing that I feel I can't do.

If making a bomb, then I know the necessary literature would be at my disposal. Gradually wisdom comes, which is most precious and must be earned. I've done all that I can do to be a good citizen, done all that I can do to ensure that I progressed with society. Intellectually, I have. Assured to be even smarter in ten more years, crooning as the knowledge that I consume in the coming years will be paired with the knowledge that I presently possess. This capacity to learn as a result of going to high school and college is a tribute to my struggle. I wanted to be smart, to speak well, so this high-octane intellect is present in you also, only needing nurturing by you. Constant reading. Constant learning. Constant inputting into your memory bank so that when it comes to the wretched seeping of the mind, the answer to your problem will be at your disposal. It's like putting money in the bank. If you don't have anything in the bank, you can't take anything out. The same goes with terms and knowledge. Put it in. You can get it out when you want it and when you need it!

Silent Intentions—Mute Destiny

Who am I, and when will I be that dream guy? This is a question that I have asked myself for years and years. At this time, I'm beginning to see who I am. Confidently, feeling a lot more comfortable with who I am, therefore thoroughly prepared to do God's will. As I continue to write in silent. No one knows Skip Flanagan. No one cares who Skip Flanagan is. Who am I? What is my destiny? I no longer look at my destiny negatively. I'm in a position to be one of the greatest individuals of this time, positioned to make the history that I dream about, positioned to make the history that I write about. I now know my destiny.

Tonight was a special night for me. I decided to take off today. I went to get my haircut, then I went to the newspaper headquarters next door. They promised me that if I subscribed to the magazine, they would do a story on me. I talked to Daryl Scott, and he is going to handle the CD. I guess it was a good day after all. I talked to Mr. Kipperman at the pawn shop, a legend in our neighborhood. I was really enjoying myself while having doubts about a lot of things. My lawn service was quickly dwindling for no apparent reason. In spite of that, I keep on going, pushing until I'm at the top. Honestly, what is the top?

After close scrutiny of my business, I've found that without a business loan, I will forever be working for my business. Also, given my client base, I'll forever be doing some form of work. I keep pushing. I have come to the realization that I'm no longer needed in the community. I'm needed in public service. I need to assist in making this world a better place, and that won't be by working for myself even though I will continue to be an entrepreneur. Undoubtedly, it's time to do greater things. Those things cannot be based on my concentration in the community solely. The purpose and intent are deeply implanted into the residents in my community. The success that is destined is yet to be seen. Although the actual benefits that were sought are evident everywhere. I'm sharp enough to now understand that the calling for my services are sought at a higher level.

I have serious concerns for my community, serious concerns for the well-being of America. I must now deal with politics and the things that accompany politics, a situation in which I have thrust myself. A destiny that to me, as I told you, is relatively fixed; I give thanks to God. Now to thank Barnes and Noble, Amazon, and Borders, who will help with the distribution of my book. The book will open up many doors for me. I refuse to let anyone down.

The sincerity of my mission cannot be mistaken for anything else. Being the reader that I am, I bought a book today. The name of it was *World Leaders Past and Present—Martin Luther King Jr.* It's no secret that I'm fascinated with the great MLK. I envy his oratory, his accomplishments. However, I attempt to accomplish my own historical feats. Undisputedly, MLK is one in a million. I began reading the book. It had a chapter entitled "Doubts about the Church." I was amazed at the thought that for someone who was a minister, he could have a doubt about the Church. I remember listening to one of his sermons. In that sermon, he questions the Church. I was once again drawn to MLK as I bore this similarity in myself, conservatively having doubts about the Church's agenda for some years now.

I eventually gained the strength, agenda, and confidence to move on my intentions to make change in the Church. Who I am, my purpose, became clearer to me. Of course I still have some bad ways to get rid of. I will now begin to be that guy, clear on the things that I can do, pursuing those things immediately. Thank God.

The things that I have been wanting to do for years have been on my heart. God has a way of punishing you when you concentrate solely on selfish things. Even though my intent was to help my family, I guess my perception of myself was just a little too narrow. I think the Man had a bigger plan for me. Here comes his plan, letting me know that I really didn't believe. I really didn't know. I was really unsure. I was wise enough to understand that redemption, reconciliation, and peace are constants in our new fight for justice. This is a part of history that must be left behind, because we are all guilty of wrongdoing at some past point in our lives. I know that there is a sincere repentance for these evils. Still, I should sufficiently look at the result of such an evil.

The opportunity to be in a country so great. The opportunity to share in this manmade wonderland. The opportunity to assist in the establishment of a world hierarchy of democracy. The opportunity to dream and be all that you can be. After purchasing the book at the Shrine Bookstore, I walked out and headed home. I decided to stop and talk to Reverend Delaney at South Park Baptist Church. He was kind of busy, so I left him a note. I noticed a flyer stating that the mayor was going to be at a town hall meeting. I had some concerns and decided to go to the meeting.

I assumed that this meeting was going to have about one hundred people there. I was wrong. I rode up, and policeman were on horses. Police cars were everywhere. I looked around, parked my van, and got out. People were rushing in like the mayor was the pope or something. I didn't tarry either. Mayor Lee Brown was the first Black mayor of Houston. He had made history. Everyone was standing in the back. I stood up against the back wall. The mayor said that there were some seats up front. He said that we were welcome to them. Nobody moved. I decided to take advantage of the opportunity and walked toward the front to take a seat.

I filled out a questionnaire, assuming that they would call us later in the week. I was wrong. The mayor said, "Skip Flanagan." I was shocked. I had just arrived! How did I get a chance to speak? I took advantage of the opportunity and asked, "Why is it that policeman work from 9:00 a.m. to 11:00 p.m.? The night shift is failing us." I also asked, "Why don't we have the proper baseball facilities in our community?" The chief of police answered one of my questions. The second question was referred to the recreation department, and he somewhat answered my questions. I was happy, sat down, and listened to the other people ask questions. I patiently waited until everyone was finished. The session was over, and it was time to leave. I decided to talk to the panelist.

I conversed shortly with Chief Bradford and then with Mr. Spellman. Last but not least was the highlight of my evening. I looked over to where Mayor Lee Brown was conversing with some of the guests. I waited until they finished. He looked at me, smiled, and reached out his hand. I reached up to shake his hand, commending him on his job thus far. I then asked if he would assist me with the one million American march. He answered, "I would love to. Get me something in writing." I promised him I would, shook his hand one more time, and left. I don't take subtle miracles like this for granted. I definitely felt in place. There was some undue respect granted to me. I could see and feel it. I knew that I had a place in this room. I deserved to have a place in this room, and police chief was not that spot. Housing development was not that spot. What was that spot? I'll keep thinking about it. I know. I also know that this was God's divine order for me to be here.

Now, I'm a real fan of Mayor Lee Brown as I see his agenda and the implementation of some of his solutions to our communities' problems. As a part of the solution, I see how he can help me, and vice versa. God's order is smoothly coming into existence as a result of all his warriors and workers. It is enough for me to believe even more in the capabilities of God, being even more inclined to be a doer of his will. Thank you, God! There is no one greater.

As we approach the last days of judgment, I can only look out and observe the nature of America, a country that is collectively sorry for the ills inflicted on its victims. Regretfully, I see the possibility for the repeat of these ill doings. What will happen if the world doesn't end? What will be the fear to do right? God is what I fear. My intentions to do right don't allow me to join forces with those organizations that I consider to be facilitators of wrong. I choose to assist in the change in a country that is dry and stagnant on beliefs, agenda, and intentions.

I certainly know the consequences of failure, and the rewards for doing God's will. Young, but fiercely thrust into situations that call for acquired wisdom; lots of knowledge. Quagmires that stem basic concerns for me and people in my community. My intentions are to be a politician, a minister, a leader, a world leader. I leave my destiny up to God. I'm not capable of the establishment of this. I'm just a player in this. He is the owner and coach. I just pray that God allows the rest of my days to be happy ones, even though I know they will be challenging. I know it won't be easy; pushing forward. I've come too far to turn back, a former selfish individual as a result of merely wanting to ensure my well-being. I have to put myself in the hands of God. I must allow Him to add the rest to me. I see clearly the problems must now implement the answers. Right now. The wait is over. To hell with the materials. My intentions are to do what is right. My destiny is public service.

Curse or Consequences

When one thinks of the possibility of hell, one has to look at what would grant one such a trip. One then begins to wonder if one is already cast to hell. If one believes that one has, it will be easy to go out and do the devil's will. That will contribute to the destruction of America, to all. Peace of mind is definitely necessary during such tense times. Justice must first be rewarded by the facilitation of information; this information must be received pleasantly, welcomed and followed by fruitful actions to bring about peace.

Wholeheartedly, someone has to bring this message of truth. Some movement must be enacted in the midst of all the hatred and bigotry. Moreover, we are all in a crisis that warrants immediate attention and immediate dialogue. Dialogue with citizens and religious leaders. God must now intervene and be a part of the solution to this new world dilemma. One has to consider the rewards for doing that which is right. Otherwise one must suffer the consequences of one's evils. As the casual observer, I now observe how African Americans must buy into the system of education and economic prosperity. African Americans can't continue to play the blame game.

Regarding this state of confusion, nobody knows why. Nobody understands the hierarchy to success. It is a simple hierarchy. That hierarchy is God, you, family, education, and job. Happiness falls somewhere in among the five. Every once in a while, poor means poor. Nonetheless, the important thing I see is that the burden of failure must fall on some group for blame. Failure in America can easily be a stepping stone for success. America allows your failure to be something that you are allowed to do. I don't blame anyone for my failure. I simply look at it as if it were a hard life. Life is difficult. I am strong. Confusion. Civil unrest. Uncertainty about the presence of God. Doubts that bring about the need to do something or find an answer for.

Self-esteem. Everybody wants to be important to someone. To friends. To family. To the community. To the world. Negatively or positively. Unsure whether there is a heaven or hell. I guess one might say I killed that cat. I guess life is life. I won't go to hell if I kill a bunch of humans. I still have the chance to be in American history. This is a choice. This is a result of the trends in the community. I'm just a young citizen attempting to prepare for my life as an adult. I'm not sure of how my life will end, yet I'm ready and positioned to make the most of either side.

I often sit and think, seeping my mind and trying to figure out my place in this life. The establishment of this place is hard in a competitive world. Success is what I'm after. A success that is weighed on the accumulation of materials. A success that is dependent on public opinion. I believe that I'm successful. When I look at all the people who are incarcerated, I praise, "Thank God." I'm glad I'm not among them. When I think of all the evils of the world, I look and praise God even more: "Thank God." Yet we live in this world. The same world that establishes the laws and rules of this land. Laws that were implemented with the intent to bring about justice, to encourage honesty, and all the terms that can be associated with righteousness.

Commonly, the results are taken wrong, and the effects are usually disastrous. In my opinion, this is why there must be changes in legislation, and also the participation in politics by all Americans, by all minorities. This will ensure that the purpose of the implementation of certain legislation can be relayed to citizens in the community. I once again must reiterate the importance of all Americans participating in the hierarchy for success. That hierarchy is God, you, education, family, and job, and happiness falls in between each one of the stages of the hierarchy at different times in your life, though not all the time. Now, add higher education and the participation in issues that concern one's self and one's family.

Last is the thought that you may be the beneficiary of bad

legislation. Cancer and other sociological ills make one consider the possibility of a curse and make one totally dependent on the unknown. The effects of evil must be countered by the unknown. That unknown is God. Carnally, some of these things can be eliminated by the accumulation of wealth. This accumulation is possible by inheritance or work. The establishment of one's self-worth falls solely in the hands of the individuals. Self-esteem. One's friends and peers are also participants in this establishment of being a worthy citizen, a valuable citizen, void of the predictions, surveys, or trends. Even so, my experiences and my knowledge shows me that education, specialization, and creation are the keys to the riddance of this curse.

As a citizen, and as Americans attempt to find their place in this country and in this world, one has to participate in the hierarchy for success. Everyone must also follow the laws in this land to establish their self-worth and find their place in the sun. There is no sympathy for past wrongdoings, just consequences for failure. Consequences once seemed unjust as the result of lack of knowledge. Now it is more understandable and maybe even supportable, and we now understand the intent of the implementation and existence of laws. This is the country of dreams. This is a country in which failure is also an option, an option reserved for any of our citizens. So whom do you blame for failure? No one. Simply accept the consequences of not trying to get rid of the curse. You cursed yourself by quitting on life in America.

Whispers of Freedom

Something keeps saying, Skip, you are free! Something keeps saying, Skip, you can be a politician. Something keeps saying, Skip, you can be a minister. Something keeps saying, You can play basketball. Something keeps saying, Trust me. Something keeps saying, The end is near. Something keeps saying, Don't trust anyone. Something keeps saying, It's a trap. Something keeps saying, You can't. Someone keeps saying, You are a fool. Watch out! Something keeps saying, Go away. Something keeps saying, You are a failure. Regardless, I keep trying.

Good or the forces of evil? Never would I doubt them. Some things that are said require attention. Some of those things require one's addressing. Any sane person would consider the things said. Optimistically, one must consider collective opinions. One must entertain the thoughts of other homelanders and people around the world. One has the God-given ability to participate in the solution or offer opinions that might be of help to these problems. The media is a powerful outlet of information. It is a way that we weigh ourselves.

We measure our accomplishments against those on TV. We measure our accomplishments against the neighbors; encountering racism along the way. This throws your thinking back for a second, makes you consider those things that are negative. It urges you to reconsider your stand on diversity and democracy. I have to keep going, keep promoting diversity, while listening to those things that are positive; I have no use for negativity.

I find that with this new God-given ability to bring together all the people in America, I cannot deny myself the opportunity to unite a country and a great culture. It is truly my intention to make this country one of the greatest in the world. As we eliminate poverty and rid our communities of drugs, we are positioning ourselves for one of the greatest challenges in this new world: the successful distribution and accumulation of real wealth. Poverty will forever exist as a result of laziness. Safety nets will be needed to aid the sick and dysfunctional, those who will not be able to function in a competitive society.

America is forever changing and will be very competitive. Who and what is America? This will be established in the new millennium as the result of unprecedented research, which will now be executed for the well-being of humanity, for the well-being of America. It is a tough task for anyone. Argumentatively, I believe that through awareness and visualization, something of this nature is easy. I believe that I can show how freedom is alive and well. I don't know about chivalry. Even so, freedom is definitely present among the masses. I just got off the phone with Sergeant Edwards, the night sergeant in our district. I made a comment in regard to a recent string of burglaries in my neighborhood. I think the other sergeant took it the wrong way. I guess given the tension and all the scrutiny that the police have been under, my statements can be taken the wrong way. I guess given the source of such a statement, the intent may be taken the wrong way. Black guy. Young. Police. I've observed the policing in my neighborhood. Some police play dirty and have been victimizing others for years. Justice will catch up to them. I remember this police officer named Peanut. Justice caught up to him. When the drug war was first recognized and acknowledged, there was a sense of urgency in wanting to rid America of the problem. Drugs were considered the worst evil in the world. Task forces and other departments were constructed to help counter the undesirable effects of drugs. I fell victim to this war a long time ago—not for a long time, just a short period. To me, drugs and bundles of money weren't reasons to give up my place in heaven. I let go of drugs.

Now, being on the other side of the fence, I can see what is going on. I'm not going to sit here and say all law enforcement officers are good. But the majority of them are. They have jobs.

These are jobs of prestige. Vividly, can you imagine being a good cop? I could. Letting people go. Helping citizens. Serving my community. Willing to take the chance of dying in my community. I think of how some deserve to be incarcerated. They are vicious individuals. How would we capture them if it weren't for the police? What about robbers? Police are definitely a welcomed sight in the community. Justice is found somewhere in the riddance of our neighborhoods of criminals and the teaching of life skills to offenders, which will enable them to participate in the American dream.

We have successfully completed stage one of this war. Now it's time for stage two. Stage two is clearly showing how the launching of educational programs and the rekindling of the American dream in all those who are misled and are outcasts is essential in one's attempt to justify the great Martin Luther King's statement, "Free at last!" For one time in my life, I was happy to hear from a law enforcement officer. I didn't have any fear because I've come to the realization that I am a citizen. I had full knowledge that he is also a citizen. Justice is one, and dialogue allows for problems to be solved. Leaders initiate the contacts and further the dialogue. Together, all components of the community make the community better. Most important is the ability to clearly see and understand how one fits into this community. This is the only way that they can see those things that are necessary for success or failure. Once they have recognized their failures, then they can clearly observe the possibility of success, never again questioning their freedom.

Then they can go fishing or jogging. Turn on their favorite tune. Jog for as far as they wants to go. Stop and fall down. Quit. Leave. In America, all of these are choices. You are free to go as you please. Don't listen to those whispers. You know now.

I Laugh; I Cry

Success is the eclipsing of a level that one dreams of. Success is fulfilling mini goals in preparation for greater goals that lead to the completion of one's greatest dream. Success for me is having all the things materially and spiritually that this life can afford me. Right now I'm standing strong in a position where success is right down the road. Yeah, right down the road. To me, the process of writing is treated just like God and the things of God. It can easily be tainted or taken wrong if you take things for granted, if you are not consistent. Life is hard for me. Each day I'm faced with challenges. Most of the challenges are material challenges.

Most of them are challenges that I can overcome over a period of time. Right now I'm kind of happy. I smiled a lot yesterday for many reasons. I had completed a project that looked much better than I expected it to. I guess some people don't know that I need to be patted on the back sometimes too. I'm not rich; I just work a lot. I'm not sure I will ever reach the monetary level of which I am due, but I keep trying. I don't think anyone knows how hard this life is for me. I know now that it is just as difficult for others. Anyway, I'm going to be kind of selfish here. What about me? Still, I'm a fan of America continuing this battle.

I got a letter the other day. It said that my book was going to be in twenty-five thousand bookstores. That made me jump up and down. I didn't know how to react. Here I am, a guy who will have at least twenty-five thousand dollars next year. I thought hard about quitting my day job, and I stopped working for about two weeks. It took about that long for me to come down off this high that I was on. I couldn't believe what was going on. This is definitely how I dreamed it. I guess now I was waiting for some type of tragic end.

I'm comfortable now. I've accepted the fact that my hobby is now going to make me rich. I was real scared because I wanted to make all the money before I put all the issues front and center; it doesn't matter. The world is just going to have to accept the fact that I'm a good writer. That's why I wrote this second book. I guess this book legitimizes me as a good writer. What do you think?

This is something very new for me—depending on public opinion. Putting my destiny in the hands of other people once again, believing that people will receive my message with open arms. I know they will feel my pain. I'm not old yet; my life can still have some relevance. Opportunities are still out there for me. So what is the problem? Not knowing what the days ahead will yield.

Those days that I have yet to see. Those days that I can see clearly as this one citizen. A citizen with diverse thoughts. Thoughts in my opinion that were commissioned by God. I'm comfortable with these thoughts; hopefully they'll keep coming. Knowing that God has millions of children, all of which will be glad to receive this good news. I can only thank God for using me, with him being my reason to smile. Unfortunately, I have to experience and witness every day the evils of the world, so I must come back down to the realities of the earth. Why do people do wrong? Why do people kill? That is something so scary to me, something I hope I never have to do. Piously, I know I'm capable. This is what makes me cry. I know that everyone won't rejoice in my success. Instead, they will use this as justification to continue their evils—and maybe even kill me. This scares me, and I have fear of the evil unknowns.

I try to look at this world in terms of perfection. In terms of my own life. In terms of my own suffering. I assume that people handle their problems the same way as I do. No, stupid. So now I'm back to block one, once again wondering. Once again curious of what lies down the road. All is rather calm right now. Just wait. I know about the other side. This is just the tip of the iceberg.

I cry because I want the best for myself. I cry because I want the best for my family. I cry because I want the best for my kids. I cry because I want justice. I cry because I want to believe in America. I cry because I don't want there to ever be racism. I cry because I don't want there to ever be killings at abortion clinics. I cry because others cry as I do, and others cried before me.

My heart is a soft one when thinking about the state and plight of other compatriots. My heart is like cotton candy and just melts away when I can't reach others. My heart is pierced because everyone is not receptive to my strides toward change. My heart hardened at the senseless death of young Americans. I cry again and again. The tears are sometimes placed on hold as I accept another call for help. I listen attentively to all the concerns of these Americans. By not yet being positioned to do anything to render aid, I can only cry. Silent tears and useless vents of anger can be registered only in my journal. Who? This specific guy who has taken on the immense task of initiating peace in our community and in this world. I see clearly, though I'm not even able to relay these thoughts to my closest of friends. Their minds are not advanced enough to be able to see the long-term intent of my actions. Their ears hear, yet their hearts harden, and the love that has been directed toward them now slides off like skates on black ice.

After crying, I laugh because I know I have done what God would want me to do, and that is to inform them. No matter what the world might say. I laugh and smile as I reach out to the world. I smile as I reach out to the community. I smile as I reach out to the world because I know if you have gotten this far, you will go all the way with me. To the end. The end, which is the beginning. The beginning of something great. You are now better off. You have now eclipsed a new level of thought, added a small piece to your repertoire.

I laugh, assuming responsibility for laughter at this one time being in your heart. I smile, knowing we are one with God. Equal in God's eyes. You feel me. Hey, you! What are you doing? Keep reading. Hey, where are you going? Tell your boyfriend to go away! Tell him you are doing something. Hey, you, don't get lazy now. I'm tired too. I guess we can all go to sleep. Go to sleep and dream. Yeah. You didn't read the first book? What is wrong with you? You're missing it. Hey, stop crying. Hey, you laughing? If not, just put a smile on your face for me. Peace. A reason to laugh. Also a reason to you know now.

All together—cry!

I Believe in Justice

I guess now is, and will be, the most difficult time in my life. I dare not fall into the same trap that got me into this mess. Public opinion. Listening to my peers. Listening to people who really don't give a damn about me. Once again I am positioned for success. Once again I have to go to so many different extremes to prove that I am worthy of reaping the rewards of my efforts. I'm in danger as a result of simply being talented. Once again I have to prove that I am that type of guy. I must repeatedly ask myself, "What is the reward for a peace seeker? What is the reward for someone who wants peace? What do I have to do?"

I now see that everyone must be happy with one's state or condition. I see that no one is concerned about the well-being of the future generations. I perceive that fear has run off all the potential followers who would have been in support of these same issues that I'm in support of. I have to be that leader that I dream of being. I must accept the fact that not only must I bear the burden of scrutiny for my thinking, but harsher consequences will accompany my actions. (I know this will be difficult for my female partner.) I now feel even more confused. I read again and again the things that I have written, seeing how truthful and sincere these truths are. I see the pain.

I was truculent, and I remain the recipient of all the wrongdoing. This wrongdoing makes for good reading. It's over now—or is it? These changes will continue to demand my time. Seemingly, these truths will forever haunt me. Many thoughts about America. Many thoughts about my community. These thoughts hurt me. Sincerely, I simply have done what I thought would be best. That was to shop my product elsewhere. The truths will once again become evident, even via the Internet around the world. I believed that everyone wanted to have peace. I believed that no one wanted to go to jail. I believed that one should reach out and show love. These are things that will not be happening in this millennium. I guess I've outlined the policy for the new millennium. I believe that once people sit back and take a look at what I have written, and the intent of my writing, they will be able to weigh the sincerity of my writing.

Small minds definitely won't be able to see the things that I see. I always say that a knife can be used to cut steak or cut throats, depending on what state of mind you're in. The majority of individuals that I know are in a different state of mind. I guess that is why everything is so segregated, why there is so much division. This is what they want. I suppose if everyone is OK with it, then cool. I'll leave the old dogs alone. So what is right? Right would be to continue to promote rap lyrics, and to continue to sell drugs with my friends.

Right would be to hang on the block and blow a big blunt with the homies to prove that I was down. No, right would be to go to the high schools and holler at all the little girls. No, right would be going to all the clubs and drinking a whole lot of liquor. Or maybe right would be being pro-Black. Maybe right would be being a militant Muslim. Maybe right would be going to the radio station and talking about a bunch of drugs and codeine. This is right for some; this is not me.

What would be right? Right for me would be going to a high school and becoming a coach. Right for me would be being a city councilman. Right for me would be working with Lee Brown and observing, as I position myself to become a politician. Right would be preparing myself for this miracle that has already taken place. Right would be positioning myself to try out for the New York Knicks or the Houston Rockets. Nevertheless, I've been in Houston for years, and the opportunity has not arisen. I guess the New York Knicks is now more realistic; this way, I can view the East Coast. I know this will be a treat. I'm almost on my way. I think back and try to find justice. I found it in Oregon. I must retreat back to the truth. What do they want—a lie?

As I get closer to my dream, I see that I must stand alone,

as I have been for so many years. Alone. Thus, I'll go into this next battle alone. Sitting here calmly waiting on the help from my fellow citizens, constantly being shut out. I already received the go-ahead. I simply have to position myself to receive the blessings. I believe. They can't believe. I guess they don't want to believe when they're not the recipients of the blessing.

So what would be justice? Justice would be for everybody to sit back and watch as I assume my place in history. Trust me, because what I'm doing is new. Trust me, because what I'm doing is right. One who is going through so much, who has to endure the hate of so many, allowing the truth to take me where I need to go. I must wait now. I don't care; I've been cautious. I've been true yet very tired. I can now wait once again to be on top. Success to me is being able to simply eclipse a dream. I know once I get to the top, I have to brace myself as the forces of evil crash into me like other bumper cars.

Waiting to be brought back down to the low level, listening to the criticism, hearing how I need to do more, hearing how I should be doing more. I know I've given lots of energy. I have given lots of love. Contentiously, without the materials this is not enough. What about the money? That's what everyone else wants. They want money. They want to see the materials. If you don't have the money, they want you to shut up. I had it; I should be able to get it again. Oh, well. I won't complain. Justice for me would simply be people and institutions doing what is right. That is understanding the plight of urban neighborhoods. Assisting in the change and investment that is necessary to ensure economic stability. Justice for me would be for everyone in America to be American. Justice for me would be to be a recipient of the love and kindness that is deserving of someone who has fought for so many other Americans, for someone who is fighting for America.

To Be Happy

As an American, I know that we live in a competitive society. I know that we have access, so we want all that this life can afford us. While living in this time where there are so many reasons to believe that the world is about to end, I know that life is hard and that the finer things in life require hard work. As an American, I know that there are many people from many different countries. America is diverse, so the possibility of someone struggling in other races is a real possibility. Because I'm smart, I know that everybody wants to be happy.

Happiness. A feeling of contentment and joy. A feeling that one gets when everything is going well. A feeling that one has that is good. A feeling that can occur for long or short periods of time. A feeling that may come and go. A feeling that is usually justified in physical representation by a smile. A feeling that anyone can have. A feeling that is the result of accomplishments and/or success. What makes you happy? What makes you happy may not make me happy. Happiness for some people is usually the purchase of some material possession. Happiness for some is love.

Often, love is received from a partner or from a family member. Happiness for some people comes real simple. For some it's just the thought of being alive. Happiness for others is having all the bills paid. Happiness for others is the absence of stress. The completion of goals. Listening to music. A combination of all of the above. I guess being rich would make anyone happy. This would definitely relieve a lot of stress and purchase tons of material possessions. This is what everyone dreams of: plenty of materials. Lots of money. Money that definitely can buy you love. Just kidding. If not, it can buy you all the things necessary to make love and eliminate the possibility of hate.

In a material society that is based on money, pursuing happiness and being happy is a difficult task. What would make me happy? I can look back and evaluate all the things that I wanted to accomplish in life. I wanted to publish a book, I've done that. I wanted to play basketball, and although tainted, I did that. I broke two records, made history! I'm positioned to make history again. I have two exceptional daughters whom I love. I've renovated my mom's house. I have paved the way for my nieces and nephews to enjoy life. I have denied myself for others, by helping and assisting others in finding their place in this life. I have now detailed a plan to perfect our country and assist in change around the world.

I have indirectly changed the way business is conducted in my neighborhood. I have also assisted in the fulfilling of God's will. That will is to have peace, to help those in need and those who have been misled. I have given a lot. Yet what would make me happy? Happiness for me would be for there to be no killing. Happiness for me would be for all individuals to participate in this life as first-class citizens, thereby raising the standards and providing a competitive society in which I would definitely excel.

Happiness for me would be for there to be no diseases and no cancer. Happiness for me would be for there to be more Black billionaires from my region. Happiness for me would be seeing racist extremists take off their mask and become united with all who love this country, giving up their hateful ways. Happiness for me would be for Muslim extremists to accept America and begin a process of reconciliation, to accept the contrition that is offered and begin anew. Happiness for me would be traveling to Israel. Happiness would be being able to go to Jerusalem and learn more about Jesus and all the prophets of God. Knowing there will be discussions of how America has done wrongs around the world, I would ask only how we could make these wrongs right. Now is a different time, the time for peace. Competition also begins now. There is a realization that life will now be a struggle and that years must be invested into oneself and one's family. This realization must not be looked on unjustly but as a crisis that will be conquered over time.

The implementation of democracy and legislation has been shown to work in other countries. Learning from legislation that has not worked. Now making a model system and implementing a government that encourages unity. This allows for diversity and further allows for unlimited economic gain. Marginal social programs with limits. Two years on, two years off. Global insurance plans that afford people cheap healthcare. Respect for individuals' means by which they establish a relationship with God. This is what would make me happy. A dream world like that. What would I be doing? Of course I'm an entrepreneur and a peacemaker, so I would simply be traveling in my own private jet.

Vacationing with Halle. Frequenting the red carpet and viewing the world with her. Encouraging her to keep her hair like it was at the Emmy's. Enjoying her while this fantasy lasts, because one is never sure of the duration of happiness. Treasuring this love that I will be giving because she is the only one who will be the recipient of this type of love. It is love that I choose to give. She is the only one who inspires me to do the things that I will do for her. Swimming in creeks. Going in caves. Everything and anything that this life has to offer, we will experience it together. Note—or someone similar to her. Smile.

Dreaming with her and being with her is the most finitely perfect occurrence to ever seep through crevices of complex thought. Isley Brothers in the air, jammin' "You're All I Need." And I say, "And I love you! Oh, yes, you are!" I go back to camp for the New York Knicks. I miss her for a little bit and then venture on a one-month vacation to do some more writing about my experiences overseas. Pictures, of course. Music, of course. I journey home to my mom's house. I go to my house in Houston and pick up my Rolls-Royce. Jammin' Isley Brothers' "Atlantis." I'll always come back to you. No worries. No stress. Just doing something that makes me happy. Riding in fancy cars.

I have done all I can do for everybody else. Now, what about me? This makes me happy. Riding. Listening to music. The air-conditioning blowing. Bulletproof. Me, one deep. Realizing that this is a material world, and none of the things that I have accomplished would have been possible had it not been for my ability to make other's money. Selfish I am not, so it's OK. Love there is not, because this love is based on the very thing called money. Yet I feel these loved ones will never be able to accept this one day of selfishness. Even though I earned it. Even though I initiated it. Even though I gave a lot of it. Happiness is something that always escapes me. Therefore, I will enjoy this day like it is my last. Enjoy it like I should.

I'm smart enough to know that happiness does not last long. This short moment that has fallen on one of the levels, or in between one of the levels in my hierarchy for success, I must cherish because when it's over, I have to prepare for more work. Public service. Political office. Another one of those jobs that pays little and requires lots. A job that may even cost you your freedom, may even cost you your life. However, in this world my life will always be in danger. That's just the nature of things. I'm a good guy who just wants to be happy. Happiness that I must initiate, facilitate, and create.

Suburban vs. Urban

I like to say that I'm an urban individual with suburban intellect. I like to discuss the problems. Yet I am very happy. I took the initiative years ago to do what it would take for me to ensure I would be prepared for this life and the workplace. Most of my friends did the same things. So what is the problem? You see, if there were no problems, then everyone would be attempting to work and be productive. What is the problem? I understand the importance of establishing a career. College was one of the most important things that could have ever happened to me. College allowed me to be the real me. It allowed me, this urban individual, to associate with other suburban individuals. These associations were important.

I once thought that Blacks were the only important individuals in society. I looked at life through the eyes of my friends. I looked at life through the eyes of my role models and leaders. When I was growing up, Harriet Tubman, George Washington Carver, Bill Cosby, O. J. Simpson, and many athletes were my role models. Nowadays, urban individuals admire other urban individuals. They idolize dope dealers and mobsters. Times have changed. It was everyone's dream to one day be like Dr. J or Tony Dorsett. Everyone wanted to speak intelligently, just like the athletes. Everyone wanted to be respected and loved. Everyone wanted the best things in life. Everyone wanted an education. Our parents fought for the right to acquire an education.

Now, what is going on? Let's take a look at the urban neighborhoods. Crime is busting out of the seams. There is a constant attempt to rid the neighborhoods of drugs, so there are constant raids and high-speed chases throughout the neighborhood. People are constantly being robbed. There is no way to get a meal. No one is working. People are stealing from each other. Everyone is an addict now. People are addicted to codeine, LSD, or cocaine. The sellers are even addicts. An addiction is a sickness. You are a consumer of something. Myself, I'm an observer of all the madness. When people are under the influence of drugs, they do things contrary to what is normal. They rob, kill, and do other things that may land them in jail. Illegal activity, this is called. Do you understand now? If you are constantly engaging in activity that is unlawful, you encourage the constant harassment by law enforcement.

High school dropouts, convicted felons, and dope addicts all reside in the urban communities. The hood. Suburbanites work, and they understand the need to have a career and generate capital. They capitalize on their opportunities by investing in locations that are free of crime and unlawful activity. These are usually intelligent individuals who have either been to college or are presently in college. These are productive individuals that are a part of the workforce. These are further locations that franchises want to invest in and look to for business opportunities. Me, I'm just an urbanite who makes money and operates a small business in an urban neighborhood.

I dream of one day moving to the suburbs. I hope and pray that one day I make enough money to do so. I don't think the majority of the individuals in my neighborhood know that I went to college. I don't think they understand the importance of attending school. Suburban residents live differently. They go to the movies. They take vacations. This is a totally different lifestyle compared to the lifestyle that inner-city individuals are accustomed to. It's a safer lifestyle. When you are in the urban neighborhoods, you have to worry about car jackers. You have to worry about thieves. You have to worry about jealousy. Jealousy may cause a fight or something.

There are so many things that can cause you to have a near-death experience in an urban neighborhood. Strangely enough, this is the way that everybody wants it. Haven't you been listening to the tapes? "I'm a gangster. I sold three bricks. I know how to cook crack cocaine. Killer, that's me." Intellect is not enough to capture the attention of an urban queen, so he attempts to rule the urban world via anything that she can relate to. Via corruption and wrongdoing.

I'm a thug, if that's what she likes. I'm a murderer, if that scares you into wanting to be with me. I'm not smart, if that is what you like. I am the most cold-hearted human known to man, if that is what you desire. I am a product of this urban neighborhood. I am the dope dealer. I am the one with three baby mommas. I am the one who has never worked for no one other than the streets. I am the one who is going to hell. Is that what you like? If that is what you like, I'm the owner of this crack house. I am the brother of the previous owner of this crack house. I am the friend of the guy who shot up his mother and his brother. He did it because they were tripping. He is real. I am the guy who robbed the pizza delivery driver who just got out of high school and is trying to make ends meet so he can go to college. I'm the guy who started Ray smoking crack. I'm the reason for Johnny getting evicted. I'm the reason for Susan getting fired.

I am a product of urban neighborhoods. I'm the one who doesn't worry about racial profiling even though I'm Black. I am the one who lives in a modest home and arranged my furniture to be financed by Mattress Mac. I'm the one who has neighbors of different ethnicity. I'm the one who meets at the gym at three o'clock in the morning. I am the one who's not a racist. I'm the one who's going back to school to get my masters. I'm the one who doesn't have to worry or look over my shoulder. I'm the resident in a suburban neighborhood. There is no fancy urban or suburban way to say that there is a problem other than by saying it. In the suburbs, the problems are not as prevalent.

The crimes committed are usually petty. Yet the urban individuals will come to the suburban neighborhoods in search of the one equalizer. A couple of thousand here or there is all that it takes. Subsequently, when it runs out, the urbanite will return to the suburbs to seize a suburbanite with the hope of reaping a reward. Who knows what might be the result of this journey? No one is for sure. Sometimes this mixture of urban and suburban can have catastrophic results. Death, even. Some people like to blame the situation totally on money. I don't believe that it's just that simple. If there was a beautiful park on the east side of town, would it matter? Imagine a beautiful park. Nice swings. Lake. Basketball court. Everything.

One day was delegated for the urban neighborhood. The next day would be reserved for the suburban neighborhood. While the urban citizens were out and about, there was a fight. The fight ended with a shooting. One guy was killed; the other went to jail. The park was vandalized. The equipment had to be repaired, so the suburbanites were a day late arriving at the park. The suburbanites enjoyed nice music. Two drunk guys started fighting. They shook hands and made up. There was another fight. At the end of the day, the park was full of beer bottles. There were two wrecks. I'm not attempting to be biased or anti-urban. I'm simply attempting to show the differences and the benefits of suburban living. An intelligent person is going to attempt to be diplomatic in solving a problem. Urban guys are not familiar with diplomacy. Their loyalty to their friends or gangs may result in a couple of killings, or maybe even drive-bys.

Everything is physical. Everything is tangible. They have not yet figured out the importance of being able to reason. Long-term planning is the key to living. Positioning. Preparing for the future. Investing. Accumulating money and educating oneself. Accessing knowledge and technological advances that can help that person later in his or her life. It all goes back to the hierarchy and discipline of this life. All are essential to the peaceful coexistence of this society. There is no way to get around it. Church is the discipline that assists you in dealing with the unknown and the unseen. Knowledge and education help you deal with the known and the tangible, those things that can be seen.

Your job allows you to generate capital that will be necessary for everyday living. Happiness comes and goes. The accumulation of all the above allows you to be able to deal with the problems that will present themselves on occasion. The ultimate goal is to live a happy and prosperous life. To max out your physical potentials. To fulfill your spiritual obligations. To do God's will. To assist others. Finally, to go to heaven. No matter the location, to rid the world of the problems that exist abroad, one must have a perfect system in place that each individual country can observe and pattern themselves after. Whether you live in an urban community or a suburban subdivision, the problems and the solutions begin and end at each individual home. The perfecting of this world is a step-by-step process. Suburban or urban, they are all a part of this world, known and unknown.

Morality Meltdown

What is necessary for a society to coexist? Schools. Jobs. Civic clubs. Facilities in the community. People of the community. Together, these individuals make up the community and are responsible for the perceived makeup of this community. Schools are very important. As I look back, I can now see how important my earlier years of learning were. In junior high and elementary, I learned a lot. I was in magnet schools. Once I graduated to high school, it was a little bit different. You had to go to different teachers' classrooms versus one teacher teaching you all subjects. Foolishly, you could get away with a lot of stuff in high school. Not going to class and other stuff came into play.

The learning wasn't as detailed. You had everybody in class now—the thugs and the mentally challenged. Learning was taking place sometimes, not all the time. I also taught school for a year. I noticed how teachers were intent on teaching kids algebra and more complex subjects, and they could care less if students grasped it. In teaching, teachers look for grade disparity. They want to have a scale or a breakdown that shows A students, B students, C students, D students, and F students. Why not have all A students? Teachers find themselves trying to confuse the students. This makes teachers seem as if they are smarter than the students. You see, the teachers have self-esteem problems too. They have to compete with the students' intellect.

When I taught, I made sure that all the students felt as if they were a part of this learning process. I made sure that the kids grasped whatever lesson I was teaching. I would ask, "Everyone got it?" That's it. It doesn't get any simpler than that. Kids were dropping out of the regular classes and coming into the class that I was teaching. I had the class for the outcast students. It was fun because I had been the outcast of a lot of things myself; I could relate to them. I taught using basics. I would go right back to timetables. I believe in repetition. Timetables at the beginning of class and at the end of class. All athletes had to bring me timetables before they came to practice. I went back to nouns, verbs, and adjectives.

I used basic sentence structures to teach these kids the basics that were essential in everyday living. I didn't believe that younger kids should focus on complex things like trigonometry until they got to high school. I mean, be realistic. How many times are you going to use algebra on a service job? I believe that the things that you teach in school must correspond with the type of jobs the students will be getting in the future. Those areas of study should warrant more attention. Students should master those things, and then you can include in their repertoire more complex terms and math solutions.

Further, I believe that discipline is a problem in schools. We as humans have become too sensitive. We don't want our kids' feelings to be hurt. In school you can no longer paddle kids. They no longer can pray. So how can you discipline your kid? I believe that African American kids have to be disciplined by paddling and spanking. You see, other ethnic groups' forms of discipline are appropriate because of their economical positions. I believe that African Americans have inherited the disciplinary components of other ethnic groups, although not the education and economic position that must accompany this new form of discipline. Taking away the toys. What toys? Taking away the allowance. What allowance? Not letting you go to baseball practice. What baseball practice? No gymnastics. What gymnastics? No family vacation. What family vacation? You feel me? In compliance, the teacher has to implement fear tactics that students are now accustomed to. Teachers now spend 45 percent of their day disciplining the students versus teaching.

Until nonviolence is accepted in the community and as a culture, extreme forms of discipline must be exercised as a deterrent to crime and bad conduct. The element of fear must be deeply instilled in these kids again. Fear of something or someone. When you send them home, discipline is also lacking as a result of conforming to societies' ways. CPS considers it abuse to discipline kids in public. I believe in strict discipline when kids are young. I remember teaching at a Catholic school. I was teaching science. I didn't know anything about science, so I went home and read. I just covered what was on the papers given me. The kids listened. None of them were African Americans. It was fun. They were just like the kids at the all-Black school.

Next, I went to the PE class. Here, I was with a bunch of bad kids. White kids, Mexican kids, and a couple of Black kids. They were acting like fools. I looked. I stood up. I hollered, "Hey, we don't do that. Everybody, sit down. We have to have discipline. Everybody knows what discipline is?" I told one of the kids to stand up against the fence. I told him not to move. Of course I was hollering. I used the same disciplinary tactics I used at Wonderland. We worked on discipline for half of the class period. They finally understood where I was going: nowhere! So they conformed. The people in the cafeteria were shocked, yet they smiled. I guess they had never seen the kids so quiet.

Discipline in America should be consistent. Kids should respect elders. They will. It's when they are old enough to learn the things that negatively affect our great country that we all go astray and participate in those things that are not for the better of our country. These results are the product of the lack of disciplinary action that impeded the learning process, making this child feel inferior and left out because he feels he no longer is worthy of a place in this society. He or she must now call on the unknown for a miracle in terms of this new world being money and a means to catch up materially to the competition.

The competition that successfully conquered the trials of this life. A new challenge to be American or to be anti-American. The easier choice is to be anti-American. Church is that unknown. God is the unknown, and people must now become totally dependent. The Church is the institution that can now assist in the reestablishment of a discipline that will afford this individual one chance to make things right. Now, this student must depend on a higher power. A mediator to assist him in getting into heaven and finding happiness on Earth. Discipline and education are those things that are lacking. Those things are essential to success in America.

There are things that were thrown by the wayside. As a child, you were unable to see the importance of anything but mischief and M&Ms. I always like to say that any denomination that your parents support, you should support too. Even so, any religion that is not an organization or extremist group and uses the Bible or Koran as a basis of its teaching is an institution that I suggest to anyone. Catholics are successful. Muslims are successful. Buddhists are successful. Baptists are successful. You can be successful in your attempt to establish a relationship with God, enabling you to clearly see your place in this life and your place in this America. You can now move forward with the hope of now becoming successful.

After one has found a discipline, one must now become competitive in society. In life, being successful is not a guarantee. Making a living is not a guarantee. We have to deal with life. Life has its ups and downs. The downs are times in which you will really need God. God is the commissioner of your newfound success. He stabilizes you to take the impact of evil, like a bumper car. It's just like when a gold tomb is exposed. After millions of years, the gold and the beauty that went into the creation of such great works still exist in its original state. God is unchanging. Each discipline encourages one to be humble and use reason. I say you should respect anyone. Respecting others is a means of establishing a relationship with God and their means by which they attempt to be successful.

In a society that thinks it knows everything, we know nothing because we have not concentrated on perfecting the very thing that got us here. It is scary to an extreme. Still, it is simple to fulfill something so complex. Respect. Understanding that we are all not alike, we are all different. However, we all must coexist. Address the problems, yet be cognizant and sensitive to others. Pain is pain, no matter who the recipient is. Yet justice is justice, peace is peace and love is love in a society that no longer believes in God. Our intelligence is progressive and allows us to see more complex things we have to see to believe. The Bible tells us about faith and miracles.

The Bible tells us lots of things and has lots of answers to some of life's most complex problems. We cannot condemn those individuals who were the recipient of such high levels of wisdom and knowledge. Those surely are subject to faults. Understand that one cannot be perfect in one's assumption of things to come. One can only give an overall view or prophecy of what one can anticipate as one observes evils and moral decline. The same moral decline that was evident many years previous. The same moral decline that is present today. Confusion once again lies in the institution that God will come to get rid of. The institution that refuses to acknowledge the existence of new prophets and prophecies because their intent is to dwell on the past. This same institution and mind thinking that locks us into the prophecy of doom as we assist in the fulfillment of this prophecy.

Not believing in the prophecy of peace because our minds are too small to see how something so complex yet so simple can coexist with the existence of evils throughout this world. Just as God sent this prophecy of doom, God also sent the prophecy of peace. Either one has the possibility of coming true. Nonbelievers have to see to believe. I think three hurricanes, numerous earthquakes, mass shootings, and who knows how much more to follow should be enough. I guess we will have to perish with everyone else. As we know, there will be somewhere else. Prepare for judgement, for the countdown as a result of this meltdown, for this moral decline. Are you ready?

Coaxed into Racism

Today, one of the guys who killed James Byrd and pulled him down the street on the bumper of the truck was sentenced. It took the jury a while to come up with a sentence. They told the judge they couldn't come up with a verdict. He told them to keep trying. They finally came up with a verdict: guilty. The jury also sentenced the guy to die by the death penalty. The day previous was kind of different. Emotions were running high. People were crying. People were angry. I had mixed emotions. Yet I know fully what is going on.

When you look at this world and all the things that are going on, something like this is easy to see. When you look at how so many traps and so many setups go on in the community, you see how corrupt this world is. Why not participate in the evils of this world? As a good guy, I'm very afraid. I'm not a part of any racist group, and I don't have a racist bone in my body. I don't even have any money. So why would I be involved in so many life-threatening situations? Why would I be the victim of so much hatred? My life is a difficult one.

Let's take a look at the conspiracy theory. In the hood, the youngsters believe that there is a conspiracy to lock up all the Black guys and keep them from making money. Is this a thought that I should consider? Yes, I'm Black. Yes, I'm a citizen in America. Today, a guy was on TV who was beaten by law enforcement officers. If I had a narrow mind, I would immediately cast doubt and scream racism against the whole police force. I would team up with the extremist groups and scream about police injustice, taking a position against the whole force. Only a handful are at fault, so I must first make sure that we are targeting those individuals that were a part of this beating. Whoever their supporters are, we are also making reference to you. It is not right to accuse the whole force because there are other policeman that stand for what is right.

I'm looking at *60 Minutes* and see how the Black students at the University of Alabama interact. This is like the dilemma that I have been speaking of for years. This university has implemented a program to encourage White Americans to attend an all-Black college—something that in my opinion is necessary. All colleges have to attempt to become more integrated. Any institution of learning, be it a junior high school or a college, has to consider integration.

At this university, there has been great disapproval of this safety net for White Americans. Take a look. Social programs were implemented to ensure the well-being of all Americans. All Americans. Why is it that African Americans have gone to this social program hogging? Why is it that African Americans have become so racist? We must once again take a look at the direction in which this car was going and see where it is now headed. Rap music has become accepted as being the best representation of music. Slang is now a good distinction. How can a culture that promotes perfection and high moral standards now compromise these high standards to appease others?

In institutions of higher learning, I think that racism should be nonexistent. The settings should be diverse. Black institutions have served the needs of those who were not able to attend the predominately White universities for years. In Houston, you can take up classes at a community college to improve your grade average, and you can then reapply to the most prestigious universities. In a society where segregation has been accepted as the norm, complexities like these are in their embryonic stages. As we attempt to make this coexistence more peaceful, I believe in a lot of different things.

I am comfortable with making my own money. I have been blessed with unlimited skills by which I can live. I wonder about all the individuals in the neighborhood. I wonder about all the people I see daily. I wonder who will disappear first. I must wonder, because the state of disarray and confusion is as clear as the *Titanic* on a small coastal shoreline. I see how difficult it is to counter this new state of confusion. This war must be fought on, and by, new and more creative means. Education once again must be the center theme in our attempt to bring about change.

I have now moved to the suburban neighborhood. I told this guy how the hood is so bad. My focus was kind of one-sided. I kept talking about the problems African Americans face. I was going on and on. He stopped me and said, "Young White Americans face the same obstacles, Skip." I had to consider the sincerity in this statement. Still, my frame for reference was narrow. There was no way to prove or disprove this fact, yet I believe that he was sincere. Once again, discipline must remain consistent for all American citizens. I believe that wholeheartedly. Unfortunately, there was no way for me to go to the hoods over there and relive my thirty-two years, so I had to trust his judgement. I know that the only way we can solve the problems are to provide the same prescription for peace to all Americans. This is my intent. I see how White Americans are also fascinated with my talents, and my eyes gleam with a new sense of hope and pride, because I have hit ground on new territory. It justifies my struggle.

It is very hard to say that I care about you. It is very hard to be diverse when the African American leaders are preparing and coaxing us into racist beliefs daily. It confuses the whole community and further alienates individuals from progressing toward the perfect world about which we all dream. Most people look at a perfect world in terms of integration and interracial marriages. It's nowhere close to that. It's more about economic balance and equal educational standings for all or the majority of individuals on Earth or in this country. The existence of equal opportunities for everyone.

It is my belief that if people had equal education, then they would better understand the laws of the land. They could better appreciate this competitive system of capitalism. They could better understand their existence. This would allow for creative solutions for all of the problems of the world. Everyone could then see the importance of life. Understand the magnificence of

God. God is the silent factor, the denominator, and the mediator in this life. Uneducated individuals cannot fully appreciate the magnificence of God. To know that, one can research literature. To know that, one can relay the knowledge of God. To know that, one can assist others. We can peacefully coexist and successfully fulfill our duties to God. Yet all are smoothly intertwined so that they perfectly blend and give balance to the present and future situations.

If I were unintelligent, it would be easy for me to be coaxed into anything. It would be easy for me to be coaxed into a gang. It would be easy for me to accept the opinions of others. It would be easy for me to agree with wrong instead of right. It would be easy for me to follow the wrong leader. Although I'm educated and can now tactfully make decisions that allow me to carefully proceed through this life, I must be careful, because my character and physical body can be assassinated at any time. Yet I'm smart enough to know that I am a leader. Therefore, I set my own standards for success and failure.

I set my own standards for bad and good, attempting to make all the right choices. If the decisions are bad, I will relay the results on to you. I have to be careful not to mess up God's mission, so I consult God often. Yet temptation will forever remain. Politicians and political coups will remain. We all must continue to promote God and righteous living. Let's not get caught up in the racism. The voice of racism is usually sponsored by other silent voices, by unseen faces of hate and bigotry.

We Must Unite!

To be diverse is probably one of the greatest challenges in America. The challenge is easy for some. Some individuals stay in integrated neighborhoods or attend integrated schools. It is a real challenge for individuals who stay in the ghetto or attend predominately Black colleges. With all the rhetoric that goes on in the hood, it is easy to see why and how an individual can easily become racist. Yet with all the negative things that are said about all the individual races, how can we unite?

Diversity: the act of being different. In this case, the promotion of patriotic unity. To show different races and denominations. The nonexistence of racism and prejudice. I stand for that. Anything other than what is right is a sin. I think it is easy to see that the best thing for this world is peace and the nonexistence of those things that facilitate hatred and lead to crime and mischief. Hate creates acts of wrongdoing against others. No man or woman can escape the possibility of committing sin. Any man or woman will commit sins against God. Yet the fear of the consequences of sin humbles people.

Now, instead of committing sins, one goes the remainder of one's life attempting to rid oneself of sin and avoid its enticements. We have to find out what is important to us. We have to do that which is right. We have to build families. We have to be patient in choosing the right partner, we must. We have to work and find ourselves in this economic system. School. Civic clubs. Policeman. City council members. The mayor. Small businesses. These are all small parts of your community. We must see how we fit into one of these categories. Together, these entities make up your community. Why can't we see how we fit into these categories? This America can be so much fun with all the money—money that is hard to get. Yet it is easy to get if you are beautiful, highly educated, or skilled. Where do you fall in? Unskilled. Uneducated. Uninspired. Let's see what we can do with that *un* in those words. Let's add *-ity*. Unity. Unity once again is not supremacy.

Everyone has a culture. African Americans like sports. They like fancy cars. They like rap music. They like looking good. They like barbecue and soul food. They like church. They like slang. They like to show. They like entertainment. Mexican Americans take pride in work. They like low riders. They like Mexican food. They believe in family. They like cowboy boots and western stuff. They like hot foods. White Americans are conservative. They are health conscious. They like lots of diet foods. They believe in education. They believe in family. They like fishing and taking vacations. They like beer. They like rock music. They believe in style and luxuries. They believe in specifics and precision. So if everybody is so different, how can we unite?

Respect. Understand. See. Look. You do your thang, and I'll do mine with style and with class. Feel me! Like Lil' Keke said, "We twenty inches in the dust on the South side." It's like that. I'm anti-violence and anti-hate. I want the streets to be clean, so when I hit the streets, everything will be cool. If not, then I'll be in the Mercedes-Benz 600 with bulletproof windows. If everything is OK, then I'll be the navigator. It's whatever makes me happy now, whatever I dream. I know I have to keep my focus and do the things that God has summoned me to do. You see, right is right and wrong is wrong. You feel me? I gotta have security. I'm the enemy on all sides. I just chill. How can we counter all the hate when every time you look at the TV, somebody is trying to play the tough guy, making stuff hot in the hood. Yet he did it just for the money. You feel me? I let people make my case. If you are dangerous, then you must coexist with the dangerous.

We are trying to get along in this real world, in America. There is nothing wrong with you liking car rims; it's how you get them. Murder is a crime. Murderers belong on death row. Citizens belong out here, enjoying this America. We are going to have peace with or without all you devils. If anyone mistakes my stance to be weak, then you are definitely wrong. I try to avoid trouble. I'm scared of what I might have to do to you knowing you are a hater, so I will stay away until I am provoked. I will first try diplomacy. After that, it's a fair ball game. The ball game is what I'm scared of. I try to win. Now on the right side, I must win again.

I must now promote American ideals. I will show that when given the chance, there will be no one better than me in music or movies. Positive that will take the industry by storm. Grassroots! I have many ideas that can ensure I will be financially stable for the rest of my life. However, people still look at my efforts to promote diversity as being suspect, so I have to go out and show even more. I have to prove even more to both sides. A difficult challenge. A challenge that I welcome. Money and materials are important in this life, yet I want to be tested and ready to receive all the gifts God adorns me with. I know that all the things that are gained through mischief must also be retained through mischief. Everything that is obtained through good and through God must also be retained by those same means.

I know that one must be careful in his association with God and materials, as those same materials will depreciate and leave. By one associating God with these materials, one will then assume God has punished one. God gives one only the knowledge and energy to be able to acquire any material asset on this earth. The devil provides balance whereas one might decide to worship both, and those good things are then forfeited to the institution of good will. Sorry. Harsh, yet true. No favor. Regardless of race, creed, or religious disposition, it is simple implementation of the laws and order of right and wrong.

Accountability and consistency are the strengths of this order. It is a consistency that has been around for years, decades, millenniums. So if everything was ok, then why would Jesus need to come back? If everything was ok, why would everyone be so concerned about the world ending? There are problems that must be solved on all sides of the fence. A balance that many have rebelled against. An order that will not change. A system that many will continue to be victims of. A simple order of right. The devil has at his disposal the same material enticements as God. The enticements are created by man. Man, who was first a thought. Man, who was first a dream. Everything in existence that was first a thought. Thoughts summoned by a higher power. Facilitated by God's children.

Now it is made accessible to all that are in existence in this world. Unfortunately, the devil is also a resident of this great world. You have to summon God and trust God to lead you in the right way. We must unite. God has made accessible the knowledge that can make this world a better place. Knowledge that can allow more of a peaceful coexistence. Knowledge that was not given to just one race or just one individual. It is a movement of enormous magnitude. The coming of the wrath of judgment. The knowledge of one's wrongdoing. Now having to face the penalties for your rebellion against the knowledge of right and wrong to which you have been exposed.

You are now accountable for what you know is right and for what you know is wrong. If one could put a color on all the individuals that I speak of, if one could put a color on the intent of the recipients of the goodwill that I attempt to input into the hearts of those individuals, that color would be red, white, and blue. If one was to say the world would end tomorrow, guess what color and religious denomination would perish? All races and religious denominations that exist on the earth. Now, you put a color on that. All the people of the world regardless of religion, race, or citizenship must unite to solve all the problems of this world. Ease the tension that is now existent in this world.

As citizens of the United States, we must come together. We must coexist peacefully. We must unite with the purpose to make this world a better place. We must unite for the purpose of doing what is right in the eyes of God and right in our hearts during quiet times and peaceful moments of reflection. I guess now we need to make higher education a prerequisite for all Americans. This is the only way to progress toward a perfect world.

A perfect world that everyone is afraid of. How can we deal

with this perfect world, should it come into existence? People are maxing out their talents. Everyone has savings. Everyone has money. There is a global crisis. No, a perfect world. A world where we must then find new inventions in which to invest our monies and efforts. There will forever be natural disasters, so the need for construction will be forever existent. Jobs will remain forever. We simply have to prepare for shorter workdays and fewer workers, and add simple tasks. The money will run out, and we will have to prepare for the effects of poverty again. The system will go around and around.

I guess what goes around comes around. Black Americans have picked up on the bad habits of humanity. They have now begun to play the race card. They are now the racist, refusing to see the benefits in an integrated school. The arrogance adorns their faces as they are now the proud recipients of the American dream. The competitive drive in them becomes exclusion and hate. So is White America wrong for their efforts to dominate society? What are Black Americans trying to do? Should we be mad because Whites are the winners? Only if you look at life in terms of grouping. Only if you look at life in terms of us versus them.

It is important to be an individual. Have your own beliefs. Have your own standards for personal success. Have your own means of tolerance and acceptance. Know the purpose of education. That purpose is to have understanding. I don't know how many times I would have to tell someone about the importance of me attending an integrated American institution. I also attended integrated junior high and high schools. I've clarified my thoughts and made for favorable perceptions of individuals of other races. As a Black American, I know how other Black Americans want all of Black Americans to side with the beliefs of the majority of Blacks. Take a look at what is going on. Blacks are now the hostile ones. Blacks are rebelling against the forces or integration, choosing to remain segregated while still wanting affirmative action programs that bring economic balance.

137

Why can't we have balance at African Americans' expense? You see now? No, you don't. You still want everyone to buy into your racist beliefs, not knowing you were a racist. Years will pass before you will be able to see the racism that was so deeply instilled, resultant of previous racism. Maybe. Yet it is time to end racism. Don't you think so? Don't let any group coax you into racism. Don't let people entice you into wrongdoing. Don't let people send you to hell. Be your own person. Be an individual. Anything that helps is OK. The opportunity is there for you. Why not allow the opportunity to be there for others? You now have the task of being Americanized. Black Americans have taken pride in this fact. That's great. Yet now is the time to see how you fit in as an American.

It is time to see how you can implement solutions that will benefit all citizens. Toss out the selfishness. Toss out the racism. Damn you in America! So let's take into consideration the elimination of all social programs. Who would feel bad? Everyone would be mad. Everyone would lose. Whatever happened to unity? Black American's unity in this regard is definitely supremacy, definitely racism. Yet there are many citizens in this country who believe in it. I know the owner of BET does. I do. We all must make a unified effort to educate and communicate to all lost individuals in America and in this world the importance of education and discipline. Justice is void among ignorance. Peace is hidden in the midst of hate. We must unite to solve all the problems, past and present. This is the only way to ensure a peaceful coexistence.

Unity Is Not Supremacy

The great Martin Luther King Jr. once stated, "You don't solve a problem of tyranny by substituting a new tyranny. A doctrine of Black supremacy is as evil as substituting a doctrine of White supremacy. God is not interested merely in the freedom of Black men, Brown men, and Yellow men. God is interested in the freedom of the whole human race." I'm a relatively young researcher who grows more fascinated with the great MLK each time I read or hear more from him. I envy the great oratory. I'm conscious of the intelligence. I'm knowledgeable of the intent of his sermons and am able to see the origin of the passion and zeal commissioned in his sermons and his movement. I then think of how such a man is an enemy of his own dwelling.

An enemy to his own country. An enemy in the very place and condition where he is attempting to change and make better. I then think and compare the things that went on then with the things that are going on now. Same conditions. Different approach. Totally different as the extent of his moral conviction and educational prowess are uncompromising and not challengeable by the greatest of men. Today I must consider whether the conditions that exist warrant such challenges, whether the conditions of today warrant this type of movement. It makes me wonder whether the necessity for a cultural unity is supremacy. Yet the existence of the same problems of injustice and the conditions simply reiterate the need for this unity. Today is the time for change. I look at the new America. I was looking through *Jet Magazine*. Entertainers were asked who were their role models. A few said MLK. Others spoke of Malcolm X and Fredrick Douglass. I like to use a combination of role models, some Black and some White. I was conversing with an individual the other day, and we were engaging in a heated debate. We were talking about issues that plagued the community. I offered my solutions and also my opinion of the problems. He didn't agree with my opinion. He was irritated and blurted, "You want to be White!"

I answered, "It depends on your view of White. It depends on your associations with the word *White*. Are your associations with the word *White* good ones? Then yes." Yet I fully understood his ignorance.

Everything that is good, African Americans usually associate with White Americans. Education. Speaking properly. Having style. Having class. Being kind. Being humble. Saying, "Excuse me." This is good. These are prerequisites to the prevention of violence. Yet in the Black community, the standards for what is good take on a whole new realm. If I can physically outrun you in a game of sport. If I can physically beat you in boxing, whether professional or nonprofessional. The individual who has the most felonies. If you smoke cigarettes. The guy who sells the most drugs. The guy who has the fanciest car. The guy who wears the best clothes. The cutest guy. This is the uncompromising standard for the Black community.

Under the terms of a capitalistic society based on the circulation of US dollars, and predicated on the English language and the American educational system, the moral and monetary value of such trends would be zero. These standards for what is good further has no value and are facilitators of a new form of urbanism that has deteriorated the African American race. These are the standards for Black kids. We must discontinue these trends. These trends must change.

These new trends have carried over into other parts of society. Young White kids are fascinated with the new trends. Mexican Americans are also fascinated with this new urbanism. All kids are fascinated with the new trends. We must intervene now to stop this new moral decline. Our focus must remain on the perfection of democracy and equal economic distribution of wealth. It is not necessarily an equal distribution based on giving, but an equal distribution as a result of the equal opportunities for competitive jobs and business loans. It is devoid of unwarranted hardships, elements, and obstacles that interfere in the attempts to pursue wealth and happiness.

Happiness is the peaceful coexistence of multiple races. Happiness is the existence of opportunities and choices. The ability to accept or decline, the opportunity to pursue the greatest dream of legal pursuit of economic security and wealth, does not necessarily constitute happiness. Yet fulfillment like this was a choice, and you chose to pursue this dream, and you made the most of it, proving to only yourself that you are capable of accomplishing goals when operating at 100 percent of your mental and physical capability. That is the goal of every US citizen.

Unity means to be one. The act of having a set of values and beliefs that are beneficial and necessary for a peaceful coexistence of a group or nation of individuals. When I read this sentence, I saw that it is more complex than its original intent. The word *individual* takes on so many different meanings because each person has a separate identity. Each individual has a different knowledge for reference. Each individual has a different religious disposition. Each individual has a different economical background. Everybody is different. Yet unity is achieved by the understanding of one's differences, and also by understanding and respecting those things in which we all share a common interest. Further, those things are essential to our economic, spiritual, and personal well-being and happiness.

Now, if we attempt to put a color on this unity, we can totally destroy the essence of the premise of this whole writing. This would be due to the fact that Americans, as great as their scholarship, scientific advancements, and achievements, have yet to eclipse a universal respect for the spirituality and duty to God. We have not accepted God and his order, because man is uncomfortable with total comfort. Nothing monetarily can be gained from total peace and comfort. States of peace and normality are unwanted conditions, and plants and businesses would become the homes and dwellings of once prosperous owners of Fortune 500 businesses.

The existence of such a peace would now command lots of sleep and sports of leisure. Is this good? Is this bad? It all depends on this monetary currency. It depends on who is harvesting the food and groceries. It depends on who is supplying the electricity and utilities. I would love to witness the purchase of all major power sources by Bill Gates. We would all have free lights and phones. I want to show the compassion that this billionaire has, because he now understands the uselessness of supremacy and economic disparity. There are millions upon millions of us who find it a difficult task to accumulate hundreds of dollars. This is why it is necessary to have unity in all its facets.

Unity is necessary to establish an economic institution that competes with racism. Unity and the establishment of powerful economic institutions are necessary to compete with prejudice and balance the scale, allowing for competitive economic distribution of wealth throughout America and throughout the world. Economic unity is necessary to facilitate economic institutions that promote education and further attempt to produce first-class citizens, eliminating the existence of low-level economic communities and the uneducated. Unity is necessary to fight legislation that promotes inequality, facilitates hypocrisy, and fuels racial separation and oppression. Unity is necessary to have a unified society and allow for the existence of love. Due to the fact that love cannot exist in the presence of economic oppression, economic inequality, and racial division.

Bad is the silence when these situations exist and no solutions are presently in place to fight and eradicate these evils. Our fight to destroy inequality and racism must be constant. Unity is necessary to weigh out fear and supremacy like thinking. Supremacy thinking and the fear that results allow for bad legislation, genocide, and rebellion against unity in all its forms. Those forms are peace, economic distribution, education, and jobs.

Disunity allows for the absence of God and the presence of the devil. The devil has no place in the hearts and communities of the unified. Peace flourishes in all the chassis and hearts of those that are unified in God. This unity travels throughout the universe, as does the air through all of our lungs. Halted by bigotry and hatred. Cutting off this free circulation and resulting in subsidiary forms of air supplied by the devil. Knowing that the original air was supplied by God, and this air reaches out to so many. It is not possible or necessary to place a color on the lungs which this air passes.

Peaceful temples of perfect unity would be the appropriate title for these servants of God and recipients of unity. Do not mistake unity for hypocrisy. Do not mistake my unity to mean I exclude. My unity should not come across as being supremacy. If we are all rich. If we all have material possessions. If we all have justice. If we all have perfect health. If we all love God. If we are all educated. If we all have material possessions. If we all understand. If we all are righteous. If we all know. If we all have access. If we all have equal representation. If we all have equal access to loans. If we all have equal opportunity for rehabilitation and repentance. If we all experience love. If we understand that we share likenesses in so many different areas—music, dance, religion, and culture. Then and only then could you understand why my desire for unity could never be supremacy!

Is This A Dream?

Every aspect of my life will now revolve around my first book. They say you don't get a second chance to make a first impression. I can only hope that the first impression of me is a good one. If not, then this project and all the ones to follow are useless. I understand the economic implications of not being popular among the majority. Yet the truth is my foundation. I must rely on truth and good reasoning. My opinions will definitely not be popular. I know this. I have simply relayed my thoughts as they were commissioned by God. I visualized these thoughts, and as a result of the knowledge and skill that I've acquired, I can now put those things on paper.

Written dreams. Actual dreams. My dreams. God's will. I will assist with the implementation of God's will and the completion of my dream. My dream is to one day see a perfect world. This world is so fantastic. There are so many things that take place each day. There are so many things that occur each day around the world. I know my existence and don't take it for granted. I don't take for granted my place in history. I don't take for granted the results of my readings. I won't take for granted the things that will follow the perceptions of my writings. I can only sit here and dream. Think about the things that I have written. Now I'm having to go out and make those dreams a reality.

Now I'm positioned to do God's will. God is the greatest of dreams. This dream is most complex, because we must rely on thought as the actual viewing of this great God. It will never be possible in the way that we want to see him. We must rely on this faith that may never be justified on this physical planet. A reason not to believe in God? No. Reason to believe as he will never conform to humans. Humans must conform to him. It is complex, as we now must attempt to decipher whether our state of being is by coincidence. Complex, as we must consider whether we are cursed and question our existence. Complex, as we must consider other forms of life. Complex, as we must consider that life may exist as it does on Earth in some other different galaxy that we may never see. Therefore we have to accept our place here on Earth. We must attempt to find happiness here on Earth, in this physical state to which we now must grow accustomed. This physical state that we now have to preserve. We must conform to this planet, conform to this country. Or make one's existence even more complex.

If one doesn't, then one has created unjust hardships for oneself. One now has complicated this process of living. One must now find blame for these injustices. One blames others. God grants one chance after chance to get back on the right track. One has the right to accept or decline the help of the Supreme Being. Then one is cast into the hells of this world, which we win or lose by chance. God is our security and assurance that everything will go right. Yet one must realize that one will only be here for a short term.

One hundred years is such a small time when compared to Earth's age and existence. Excuse me, but the average life span is about sixty-seven years. No one gets to one hundred anymore. So why flirt with death and failure when life is so short? I guess one might be in a hurry to try something else because one has failed this test. Now it's on to a new sequence of events. You simply have to live this dream and take it for what it is worth. No one knows when one's life is going to end. When it's over, it's over, and you won't even know. I sometimes wonder when I see tragedies. I wonder how I died in the life previous. If so, how many times have I died? What was it like? What made me happy in that life? I wonder what can make me happy in this life.

This new dream. I now think about getting old. Running for city council. Finding a wife in Hollywood while I'm producing movies. I bring this talent back to Houston. I make Houston more star friendly. I implement laws and make changes that will make Houston one of the greatest cities in the world. I run for mayor.

I win. Halle and I have a son. I go to the ranch and take care of the kids. I work out and count my investments, then continue to flirt with different investments. Relax and enjoy the results of my efforts and sacrifices as a youth. Continue to write and make appearances. Live this life.

A happy life will be difficult. Yet every day I will consult God and therefore receive the guidance that is needed to make it through the day. Each day, each minute, one cannot take a day of this life for granted. This opens the door to mischief. I am worried that something might lead me astray of God. Life is life. We exist. Yet to someone else, all that exists is what we see, and those thoughts that we perceive are real. It's all just a dream of which we are all a part. A dream that we all have knowledge of its existence. We take so much for granted. Not me. I just keep dreaming. Keep living this dream.

Final Judgment

I guess after you look at all the things that have taken place on Earth, one must now consider the prophecies in the Bible and things that most of us discuss. The most popular are the theories that the world is going to end. Another is that the Y2k bug will create disasters worldwide. I guess we have been living a relatively comfortable life for the last ninety-nine years. Yet I believe that neither is going to happen. I believe that America has done some things for which it must now repent. I further believe that other Americans will continue to be baited into gangsters and corruption. Individuals will continue to live by mob like principles, because this less intelligent society will forever not be prepared for competition. The society will be unable to accept failure. The idea of failure will result in means of survival that won't be God-like. So is this world.

Corruption has a firm grip on the leaders of this world. If there is the existence of corruption, there lies the ability of the existence of sin. There are problems. Yet the greatest of the problems on Earth are problems like cancer, AIDS, and other diseases that affect society. I see these as major obstacles that interfere in the peace process. Further corruption and racism are major obstacles that interfere in the peace process. Other than that, everything is fine in America. People are going to be people. People are going to go through changes with good and evil. Some things will remain to keep balance. In life there are problems, but these are problems that can be eliminated with education. The existence of racial divisions are clear. The knowledge of the ills of our country stick out like dirt on white sheets. They are problems that we all must participate in the solution of. I must say when I look at people in the ghetto, a real sense of anger arises.

I know that everyone who wants a job can get a job, and those who can't work can get disability. I get angry because everybody wants something for nothing. The thought that someone is rich means that the person must now give to others. So what? The same way that he got it, you can go get it. This is why I think God let me go through the process I went through. I had to learn the process of exclusion, the process of being left out. Once again, how would you feel? No one can be left out. Each life is a precious life to someone.

We cannot look at any human life as invaluable. No one knows the level of another's personal suffering. We as individuals must simply attempt to max out our talents on this earth, as is the tradition of this great country, where all ethnic groups and races have seen some form of success at all levels of sport and work. Yes, coaxed we are, sometimes into popular thinking and popular traditions. Yet the coming of God and the realization of simple truths are now evident and at the hand of the reader. Beautiful people on all sides of the fence. A beauty that is in the eye of the beholder. Different cultures. Different places. Different destinies. We cannot be overtaken by the forces of evil. American, there are problems.

As we approach the new millennium, we now realize that two million African American males will be imprisoned. Is there a problem? I say yes. Is there a conspiracy? I say no. Should African Americans conform to the system and adhere to the hierarchy to success? I say yes. In a country that is based on talent and intellect, everyone must actively pursue this education that can open up the doors of opportunity, thereby ending this state of division and disunity. If not, then yes, plan for destruction. Unintelligent individuals will now begin an assault against good, creating evils throughout the world. The winner once again is labeled the beast. Therefore now we must reach out to solve all the world's problems and form a universal democracy. Explain the benefits of this global movement.

Teaching respect. Justifying all religions. Participating in the solutions in your state, in your country, in this world. Yes, the end is near. The end to hypocrisy, hatred, bigotry, and misfortune. I say wake up, get up. We are all Americans. We are all citizens of this world. Yes, this movement is to restore peace. Get back on the track of space exploration. Open the doors up to travel once again. Make it safe once again to go other places in the world. World, get ready for the return of God by subtle miracles. Take not for granted this goodwill. There will be recourse for global disregard to fulfill the prophecy of peace. We must have peace. We must unite. We must realize what it takes to become successful. Success is the gift to the overachiever. Not the underachiever. Not those who don't even try. Not individuals who have quit on life. It's time-out for the blame game. It's time to go out and pursue our dreams. Last, if the world is going to end, then so be it. Assuredly, I can promise you one thing: in heaven, there won't be just rap music.

How Did You Become Rich!

I guess the better question is, what was the driving force behind you pushing so hard to survive. Now that we are at destinies front door lots of questions are being asked. Lots of things are expected. All those years going to sleep dreaming of becoming Rich. Trying to figure out how to describe Rich. Trying to see exactly what and when and how can I bestow the title to my name.

I learned that that word Rich has a lot of weight. It is a word that is complex. It is a catchy word. Everyone wants to be Rich. I am an entrepreneur. I have been one for 28 plus years. I enjoy entrepreneurship. I still struggle with entrepreneurship. But my business is profitable. I have financed all my dreams with my business. I stayed out of jail and am able to watch my kids and grandkids live their lives. My business has done exactly what it was supposed to do.

My business has consumed years of my life. But I love my business. As I look at life I don't see anything else I could have done. I had to use my business to finance my dreams. I had to build a business that I loved and that I knew I could work for the rest of my life.

I always say you have to have a job to get the job. The job will finance the dream. While chasing the dream God will reward you with destiny.

I continue to believe in God. I have not wavered. Its 2021. I wrote this book years ago. But it's amazing how it remains relevant to this day. I have left a lot of content from original book in this final book. Reason being it is my truth and the lot of the information remains relevant to this day.

I think I am a lot wiser and I have confirmed a lot of things that I wrote in this book.

I guess its like when u buys a classic car you want to keep

everything original. But I kept it as original as possible. Times have changed. Presidents have changed. I have gotten older. This is all new.

I don't get to be this guy. This is a very intelligent seasoned guy. One that I see now has a God anointing. The things I write just come out fluently. I think my love of my business to go along with my fear of failing drives me.

I have been thinking about a lot of things over the years. But I am at a point of clarity right now. This chapter here is the final chapter before destiny.

This year brought in a new president. It has been tough so far. But it also brought hope my way. A new friend and publisher.

My phone rings all day. I get emails all day. About my music and about my book.

I got a phone call one day that changed my life. I've had publishers call my phone for years. I was with the same publisher for years. I think I can sometimes be loyal to a fault. I wont lie there are so many things that go on until the publishing process will definitely discourage you. So I answered my phone.

This guy was on the phone. I couldn't understand much of what he was saying. But when I did everything sounded real good. I was like wow. This is it. If this is it. Lol. So I told him to call me back. He called me back. So he asked did I read his email. I said yes. My lawyer is ex Sony Music executive and my good friend Corey Jones.

I called him I said hey man these people got some type deal it sounds good but I don't believe them. He asked what are they saying. I said they say they say they are a book endorser. He said that's cool. I said I'm going to see what they say. He said keep me informed. So Mr. Grey Allen called. He said I'm with Book Chambers. I said cool. I said I looked up your website and I couldn't find anything bad but I can be in LA next week. He said we schedule those appointments. So me being me. I was like man this cant be real. So I said my lawyer can meet you right now. He said great. I was like ooops. So I said he stays in LA. He said great. Now I was getting scared. I was like this might be the real deal. So he forwarded me to his boss. So his boss was like we need to get this thing moving. I said well you need to call my lawyer. He said well where is he. Do you have a number for him? I was like oooooooooweee. So I gave him my lawyer's number. I waited. Couple hours Mr. Allen called back. He was laughing. He said Skip did you talk to your lawyer. I said no let me call him. I called my lawyer. He said it sounds legit. I said for real. He said yes. I was like Yesssssss!!!

I called Mr. Allen back. I said lets deal. He put everything into motion. They asked me to send them book cover and everything I did. I loved my book cover. A month later they sent back a new cover. I looked at it. I looked at it again. I was impressed. It looked like a book cover you see on the buildings in Vegas and Tokyo. I was like this is the right team. It was like when you meet the right female. The chemistry was there. What could I say? If they don't do anything else that cover is amazing. So anything after that is like piling on in the NFL or running the score up in the NBA.

The cover speaks volumes. This is destiny. Destiny is unexpected. But you know when its time. The time is now. It's definitely a part of the American dream. When you do what you are supposed to do and at some point God appoints willing partners. I have more books. Good books. Kids books. This is getting exciting.

I have no reason to not believe in my new family. Book Chambers. This is something new. A company that sees something and does something mutually beneficial. I paid my dues in the little league. It was fun. But this is the part that I have been waiting for. I love music. I love my business. But writing is my destiny. Its something I do fluently. I'm excited about what's next.

I don't want to let anyone down. I always scan my brain for reasons I could let people that believe in me down. But I can only be me. I look forward to assisting with making the world a better place with my writing. I look forward to being the one that stands up for Christians and good people. I look forward to bringing people together. I look forward to telling the truth.

I believe this is the beginning of a new movement. A wake up call. A call for unity. A call to reevaluate who we are. A call to go back to helping one another. A call to help good people. A call to return to God. I just want to make people aware of the things that are going on. Then be a part of helping to fix the problem. I hope me sharing my struggles can help you. Help America. It's something new. Something different.

But they still asking how did you get rich? I never gave up. And I put myself in a position to be rewarded for being faithful to myself and to God. And a good person and company reached out to me and everything they said they were going to do they did. And I did my part and promise to do my part for as long as I live. Thanks to my new publishing Family Mark Gonzales, Grey Allen, Shawn Dawson and the Book Chambers Family!! Thanks for all you do! Enjoy!!

"Skip Flanagan, Your Only Choice Is to Become Rich"

The unselfishness that lies in me is nonexistent in others. The love that I give is given without the slightest hope that this love will be returned. Me, this kind man. Me, this God-loving individual. I, Skip Flanagan. Dreaming. Working. Pushing. Trying. People taking. I still attempt to eclipse a level where I cannot be bothered by all the taking and all the punishing. I can only believe in the One who has brought me this far: God. The allies of God and goodwill. Complex is my struggle, because I want not to create any war. Complex is my struggle, because I don't want to offend. Complex is this life, because I am a product of urban thinking. Complex is this life, because I want to be right. Complex is this process, because everyone around me is not like me. Complex my life is, because I know not how so many can worship the forces of evil.

I know not of the reasons why so many people hate me. I push on. I attempted to count the number of college grads that are in my area. There are none. I count the number of middle-class individuals whom I call friend. Once again my mind is challenged to find one. America is once again challenged to make this country perfect. I take it to be a challenge to assist in the straightening out of the minds of all misled Americans, urban and suburban, poor and rich. Individuals who have been obviously hurt by the effects of slavery and prejudice. Even so, time has come to move forward. Turn the vehicle around and steer it in the right direction. Get back on the right track. Forgive and let it be that forgiveness. Toss away the bitterness. Relinquish the hate. Go back to the basics, that which got us to this point: God. A vicious challenge to be right, always having the safety net of slavery and racism as a safety net of blame to justify your present position.

How about failure? How about you quit? It's time to let go. It's time to teach the kids love and fellowship. It's time for change. Let your heart be the recipient of this love. Cleanse your minds of evil mischief and bad past. Brace yourself for this new life in which you will now be an active participant in change. Direct all your energy toward that which will benefit you and your family. Direct all your energy toward making all these wrongs right. You can do it. You're bigger than that. Peace. You feel me? All Americans have problems—money problems. Everybody hustling to eclipse the level of just getting by. Everybody wants to be rich. Everybody wants to not work. Yet everybody has to work to get to the point of no work. Everybody must participate in the hierarchy for success. Education, specialization, or creation.

Education will remain in the hierarchy for the remainder of your life with God, self, job, and family. Happiness falls somewhere in between these levels some of the time but not all the time. There must be the existence of respect for things that you know little about. Respect for one's home. Respect for one's spouse. Respect for one's children. Respect for one's religion. I didn't say they were right. I said they had the choice of choosing. You don't know whether you are right, so let individuals find their way to heaven as long as they don't bother or harm anyone. As for myself, I'll keep researching. Keep listening. Keep learning. Keep positioning myself for greatness. This will be the last book of constructive criticism for a while, at least for two years.

I want to try my luck at autobiographies and novels. You feel me? This is going to be hard because the recipients of this message may interpret the intent differently from my perceived intention. I'll just move on and once again prove I'm a skilled writer. I anticipate every book and every day of my life as a challenge to prove that I am a writer. A visionary. A promoter of diversity. A teacher. Maybe even a leader. Who knows? This is America. That's a job. Why not me? Why not Skip Flanagan? Good jobs. Jobs that I can sleep on. Jobs that I can go home and tell my kids about.

Now, what if I were president? What could I do? What would I say? The first thing that I would say is, "Anyone who is not Black, interns included, needs to start looking for jobs." Further, we will be forming a committee to see if we can change the name of the White House to the Black House, or something more diverse. I'm just joking—no way would I fire the interns. I would lay off all the male interns and replace them with a diverse crop of single females. I would answer questions promptly and sincerely.

If one was to ask me, "Are you for abortions?" I would say no because I know there are some instances that warrant abortions. Then someone would ask, "Are you against homosexuals?" I would again say that no, I'm not against anyone. My position is that I am for a perfect world and against anything that facilitates racism. I'm against anything that promotes hatred or any legislation that interferes in any American's ability to exercise his God-given rights. I'm against anyone who is in opposition of the US constitution and the freedoms that it affords Americans. I'm against anything or any legislation that interferes in the process or does not allow for the unabated access to making millions. My agenda would be to assist small businesses and strive for better facilities for public schools.

I would form a committee to study the discipline and teaching methods at private schools, and I would immediately begin the implementation of those policies and guidelines into the public schools. I would have at least three hired disciplinarians at each school. They would be solely responsible for the implementation of discipline. I would simplify the school curriculum for elementary and junior high schools, concentrating on basic skills. I would leave high school for more complex learning as the student prepares to enter college. Students must receive an evaluation from the counselor so they can have a realistic chance of succeeding by knowing the direction that they should be headed.

I would caution teachers to be very careful and target students who seem like they are not focused. We would then put them in alternative programs. I would draw up a plan to implement a five-year, no-tax plan for small businesses with gross revenue under thirty-six thousand dollars. At the end of this five-year period, an assessment will be made. If the business has not shown progress in this period, it will be given an additional probationary period to straighten out the problems. Individuals then will be instructed to pay taxes to an office every three months, like a probation office. They will each have an individual officer. Next, I would make the government liable for 45 percent of healthcare costs.

Office visits will be free for nonworking individuals. Credit that to the government. X-rays will be 65 percent paid by the government, as would major surgeries. I would then make the balance deductible from paychecks not exceeding 10 percent of the check. I would make it where a female could get welfare for two years only. Then she must get off for two years. It is six years total for a lifetime. After that, she must then seek disability. I would eliminate child support altogether. Last, I would make a college degree a prerequisite to early releases from prison. I would also use this as a means to cut into time by 30 percent. The addition of a trade will warrant a 10 percent increase toward a deduction in time for nonviolent offenses.

For violent offenses, then 10 percent. For murder, I have to think about it on a case-by-case basis. Yes, all of these would be difficult sales. This is my agenda in full detail. As for serving ten years on probation, I must consider the effects. I must further consider the effects on less intelligent individuals. I must then attempt to simplify this process. I must make individuals aware of the problems. I must then present solutions. I must live by these guidelines. I must be this guy. I know what God wants. He wants peace. I know what America wants: diversity. I know what I want. I want happiness all the time. God holds you accountable for the knowledge that you have. He doesn't punish you for lacking knowledge. You are only accountable for the things you know. I know about this great place. I'm telling you about a greater place. I'm trying to make this time fun while it lasts. Given the things that I know and the things that I will now relay to you, I can say that I'm now about to go on vacation. I will be enrolling in school. I have to finish my degree. Being rich is an option in America. I have no other choice but to become rich!

And Now

Are you ready? they scream as they are about to begin the race.

Your heart now pumps with adrenaline; buckets of sweat cover your face.

This closed gate is the only thing that stands in between you trying.

Winning and losing are your only options, as the day has come. Perfect timing.

Thoughts of turning back as you are unsure, not certain if you are fully prepared.

Too late—the gates about to open. Your heart begins to pound, the unknown reason why you are so scared.

Many like you are positioned side by side along the way.

Winners and losers are predestined titles, as we are unsure of what this day may make.

Embarking on new territories, new horizons. The time has come. We come as one.

If we win, we will know. If not, we can look and reconsider as we count down to a new millennium.

The time has come; the gate is open. No time to think. You must compete, and how.

Everyone in shock for one moment, utter silence, and now: 2000.

Acknowledgments

First of all, I would like to thank God for allowing me to finish the many projects that I have dreamed about completing. I am most excited about the thought of how all my dreams will one day be a reality. I also would like to thank Don White and Xlibris, my publishing company, for this great miracle. I am so excited about my new job. Thanks for trusting me, because I knew my position on some issues was not consistent with yours. You allowed me an opportunity to have a voice for others to at least listen to. I may be wrong for some of the things that I have done; I am definitely not sure. Yet I simply followed my heart.

This project was difficult, yet not as difficult as the truth is an easy story to write. My ideas may be a little offbeat. Yet once again I feel they must be considered. I, an American, can now see more. I'm now a part of this change, a new change. Yet I'm not sure whether my ideas will ever be considered because economics plays such a major role in the establishment of success and failure, in living and dying. I would like to thank the individuals who do take the time to trust in me. It would be the same evil of others if I did not. I guess this is why I attempt to reach out as I do. Thanks for the voice, because the big guys with all the money usually have the last say. Thanks also to Barnes and Noble, Borders, and Amazon for assisting in the distribution of my works. Hopefully, we will be a team for the rest of our lives on the planet, for as long as this lasts. For now, thanks.

Last, thanks to all the true Americans because you are who I stand up for. In a world where it is easy to be coaxed into racism, I choose to do the hardest thing: promote diversity. I know this will be one of the hardest tasks of my life. Yet we all must wake up. Someone laid the footwork so that life could be a lot easier for you. I will now do the same as a true American. While others still battle with superiority theories, I'll move on, knowing that their intents are truly self-serving. I'm wise enough to see the direction this hate will lead. I know I could get out alone but have chosen to take others with me—others like me. I also must realize that I will now have enemies. I'm so sensitive and never want to have enemies, because I know the power of the devil. I accept. I must move on. I have a choice. I choose to be American. I accept all that comes with being American.

I would also like to thank Facebook, Myspace, and all the social networking sites that made it possible to share my writings. I would like to send out a special thanks to Tosha Dearsbone, Wendy Beckham, Lady Gee, Monica Kirkendol, Tarsha Duckworth, Portia Chandler, the Beautiful Butterfly, Boogie the king of the North, Dakeem David, and all the friends who supported me in good and bad times. Thanks for all the likes.

I would like to send a special thanks to my family, my niece Kenyania, Krystal, and my nephews Mario and Thomas. Thanks to my baby momma; you have been there in a big way. Thanks, Jason. Thanks, Doc. You are the realest. Thanks to little brother Russel Bersard and to Nate Mitchell. Thanks, Mr. Mitchell. Thanks to all my lawn customers—you are the reason! Thanks, Mr. Allen and Mr. Moore. Leo and Doc! My homies Calhoun and Dorian! Main Duckworth and Miss Lydia! Rl and Mrs. Jones and Mrs. Ruby! Mother-in-law and everyone who has shown me love over the years! D Ray! Everybody! It's been real!

To my daughters, Darina and Kayla. I love you dearly! I dedicate this book to the inspiration of my life. No one pushes me harder. No one makes me want to become rich more than you. There could be no better motivator than you. My thanks to you! All my love is yours! Thank you, Halle Berry! My first book goes to you!

More Thanks

I would like to send a special thanks to Paul Kyriazi. Thanks for sharing as would a true leader and child of God. Interviewing you that morning put a lot on my mind. I listened attentively, and one thing that keeps coming to mind is you saying you have to have finished products. I took off the whole year to finish all my products, and this is the first of those products. People like you are the reason why I am the person I choose to be. Keep planting seeds. Hope to meet you soon.

I also would like to thank George Blair, Courtney Green, both Nicks from South Acres, Russ, Jack, Elliot, Reverend Hayes, Lynn Griesmer, Michelle Boni, Holly Alfred, Alaura Stephanie, Gina Host, Ron Lewis, Cedric Tubman, Gene Hughes, Richard Faust, Sherone Vaughn, Cheryl Brown, Boute, and my fraternal brothers BJ, Carlos, and Hamilton. Mike, thanks for checking on me! Roderick Eye! And everyone who has ever taken time out to show me love. I definitely appreciate it!

Did I miss God? Well, just in case I did, thank you, God! My life has been all that I can ask. Now, on to history!